MACMILLAN MASTER GUIDES

KING LEAR

BY WILLIAM SHAKESPEARE

FRANCIS CASEY

with an Introduction by
HAROLD BROOKS

MACMILLAN

First published 1986 by
MACMILLAN PRESS LTD
Houndmills, Basingstoke, Hampshire RG21 6XS
and London
Companies and representatives
throughout the world

ISBN 0–333–40378–9

A catalogue record for this book is available
from the British Library.

12 11 10 9 8 7 6 5
03 02 01 00 99 98

Printed in Malaysia

CONTENTS

GENERAL EDITOR'S PREFACE

The aim of the Macmillan Master Guides is to help you to appreciate the book you are studying by providing information about it and by suggesting ways of reading and thinking about it which will lead to a fuller understanding. The section on the writer's life and background has been designed to illustrate those aspects of the writer's life which have influenced the work, and to place it in its personal and literary context. The summaries and critical commentary are of special importance in that each brief summary of the action is followed by an examination of the significant critical points. The space which might have been given to repetitive explanatory notes has been devoted to a detailed analysis of the kind of passage which might confront you in an examination. Literary criticism is concerned with both the broader aspects of the work being studied and with its detail. The ideas which meet us in reading a great work of literature, and their relevance to us today, are an essential part of our study, and our Guides look at the thought of their subject in some detail. But just as essential is the craft with which the writer has constructed his work of art, and this may be considered under several technical headings – characterisation, language, style and stagecraft, for example.

The authors of these Guides are all teachers and writers of wide experience, and they have chosen to write about books they admire and know well in the belief that they can communicate their admiration to you. But you yourself must read and know intimately the book you are studying. No one can do that for you. You should see this book as a lamp-post. Use it to shed light, not to lean against. If you know your text and know what it is saying about life, and how it says it, then you will enjoy it, and there is no better way of passing an examination in literature.

JAMES GIBSON

NOTE: The recommended edition to which all text references apply is *King Lear* edited by Philip Edwards in *The Macmillan Shakespeare*.

Cover illustration: *Lear and Cordelia* by Ford Madox Brown, courtesy of Tate Gallery Publications Department. The drawing of the Globe Theatre is by courtesy of Alec Pearson.

AN INTRODUCTION TO THE

STUDY OF

SHAKESPEARE'S PLAYS

A play as a work of art exists to the full only when performed. It must hold the audience's attention throughout the performance, and, unlike a novel, it can't be put down and taken up again. It is important to experience the play as if you are seeing it on the stage for the first time, and you should begin by reading it straight through. Shakespeare builds a play in dramatic units divided into smaller subdivisions, or episodes, marked off by exits and entrances and lasting as long as the same actors are stage.

The first unit provides the exposition which is designed to put the audience into the picture. In the second unit we see the forward movement of the play as one situation changes into another. The last unit in a tragedy or a tragical play will bring the catastrophe and in comedy – and some history plays – an unravelling of the complications, the *dénouement*.

The onward movement of the play from start to finish is its progressive structure. We see the chain of cause and effect (the plot) and the progressive revelation and development of character. The people, their characters and their motives drive the plot forward in a series of scenes which are carefully planned to give variety of pace and excitement. We notice fast-moving and slower-moving episodes, tension mounting and slackening, and alternate fear and hope for the characters we favour. Full-stage scenes, such as stately councils and processions or turbulent mobs, contrast with scenes of small groups or even single speakers. Each of the scenes presents a deed or event which changes the situation. In performance, entrances and exits and stage actions are physical facts, with more impact than on the page. That impact Shakespeare relied upon, and we must restore it by an effort of the imagination.

Shakespeare's language is just as diverse. Quickfire dialogue is followed by long speeches, and verse changes to prose. There is a wide range of speech – formal, colloquial, dialect, 'Mummerset' and the broken English of foreigners, for example. Songs, instrumental music, and the noise of battle, revelry and tempest, all extend the range of dramatic expression. The dramatic use of language is enhanced by skilful stage-craft, by costumes, by properties such as beds, swords and Yorick's skull, by such stage business as kneeling, embracing and giving money, and by use of such features of the stage structure as the balcony and the trapdoor.

By these means Shakespeare's people are brought vividly to life and cleverly individualised. But though they have much to tell us about human nature, we must never forget that they are characters in a play, not in real life. Remember, they exist to enact the play, not the play to portray *them*.

Shakespeare groups his characters so that they form a pattern, and it is useful to draw a diagram showing this. Sometimes a linking character has dealings with each group. The pattern of persons belongs to the symmetric structure of the play, and its dramatic unity is reinforced and enriched by a pattern of resemblances and contrasts; for instance, between characters, scenes, recurrent kinds of imagery, and words. It is not enough just to notice a feature that belongs to the symmetric structure, you should ask what its relevance is to the play as a whole and to the play's ideas.

These ideas and the dramatising of them in a central theme, or several related to each other, are a principal source of the dramatic unity. In order to see what themes are present and important, look, as before, for pattern. Observe the place in it of the leading character. In tragedy this will be the protagonist, in comedy heroes and heroines, together with those in conflict or contrast with them. In *Henry IV Part I*, Prince Hal is being educated for kingship and has a correct estimate of honour, while Falstaff despises honour, and Hotspur makes an idol of it. Pick out the episodes of great intensity as, for example, in *King Lear* where the theme of spiritual blindness is objectified in the blinding of Gloucester, and, similarly, note the emphases given by dramatic poetry as in Prospero's 'Our revels now are ended. . .' or unforgettable utterances such as Lear's 'Is there any cause in Nature that makes these hard hearts?' Striking stage-pictures such as that of Hamlet behind the King at prayer will point to leading themes, as will all the parallels and recurrences, including those of phrase and imagery. See whether, in the play you are studying, themes known to be favourites with Shakespeare are prominent, themes such as those of order and disorder, relationships disrupted by mistakes about identity, and appearance and reality. The latter were bound to fascinate Shakespeare whose theatrical art worked by means of illusions which pointed beyond the surface of actual life to underlying truths. In looking at themes beware of attempts to make the play fit some orthodoxy a critic believes in – Freudian perhaps, or Marxist, or dogmatic Christian theology – and remember that its ideas, though they often have a bearing on ours, are Elizabethan.

Some of Shakespeare's greatness lies in the good parts he wrote for the actors. In his demands upon them, and the opportunities he provided, he bore their professional skills in mind and made use of their physical prowess, relished by a public accustomed to judge fencing and wrestling as expertly as we today judge football and tennis. As a member of the professional group of players called the Chamberlain's Men he knew each actor he was writing for. To play his women he had highly-trained boys. As paired heroines they were often contrasted, short with tall, for example, or one vivacious and enterprising, the other more conventionally feminine.

Richard Burbage, the company's leading man, was famous as a great tragic actor, and he took leading roles in seven of Shakespeare's *tragedies*. Though each of the seven has its own distinctiveness, we shall find at the centre of all of them a tragic protagonist possessing tragic greatness, not just one 'tragic flaw' but a tragic vulnerability. He will have a character which makes him unfit to cope with the tragic situations confronting him, so that his tragic errors bring down upon him tragic suffering and finally a tragic catastrophe. Normally, both the suffering and the catastrophe are far worse than he can be said to deserve, and others are engulfed in them who deserve such a fate less or not at all. Tragic terror is aroused in us because, though exceptional, he is sufficiently near to normal humankind for his fate to remind us of what can happen to human beings like ourselves, and because we see in it a combination of inexorable law and painful mystery. We recognise the principle of cause and effect where in a tragic world errors return upon those who make them, but we are also aware of the tragic disproportion between cause and effect. In a tragic world you may kick a stone and start an avalanche which will destroy you and others with you. Tragic pity is aroused in us by this disproportionate suffering, and also by all the kinds of suffering undergone by every character who has won our imaginative sympathy. Imaginative sympathy is wider than moral approval, and is felt even if suffering does seem a just and logical outcome. In addition to pity and terror we have a sense of tragic waste because catastrophe has affected so much that was great and fine. Yet we feel also a tragic exaltation. To our grief the men and women who represented those values have been destroyed, but the values themselves have been shown not to depend upon success, nor upon immunity from the worst of tragic suffering and disaster.

Comedies have been of two main kinds, or cross-bred from the two. In critical comedies the governing aim is to bring out the absurdity or irrationality of follies and abuses, and make us laugh at them. Shakespeare's comedies often do this, but most of them belong primarily to the other kind – romantic comedy. Part of the romantic appeal is to our liking for suspense; they are dramas of averted threat, beginning in trouble and ending in joy. They appeal to the romantic senses of adventure and of wonder, and to complain that they are improbable is silly because the improbability, the marvellousness, is part of the pleasure. They dramatise stories of romantic love, accompanied by love doctrine – ideas and ideals of love. But they are plays in two tones, they are comic as well as romantic. There is often something to laugh at even in the love stories of the nobility and gentry, and just as there is high comedy in such incidents as the cross-purposes of the young Athenians in the wood, and Rosalind as 'Ganymede' teasing Orlando, there is always broad comedy for characters of lower rank. Even where one of the sub-plots has no effect on the main plot, it may take up a topic from it and present it in a more comic way.

What is there in the play to make us laugh or smile? We can distinguish many kinds of comedy it may employ. *Language* can amuse by its wit, or by absurdity, as in Bottom's malapropisms. Feste's nonsense-phrases, so fatuously admired by Sir Andrew, are deliberate, while his catechising of Olivia is clown-routine. Ass-headed Bottom embraced by the Fairy Queen is a *comic spectacle* combining costumes and stage-business. His wanting to play every part is *comedy of character*. Phebe disdaining Silvius and in love with 'Ganymede', or Malvolio treating Olivia as though she had written him a love-letter is *comedy of situation*; the situation is laughably different from what Phebe or Malvolio supposes. A comic let-down or anticlimax can be devastating, as we see when Aragon, sure that he deserves Portia, chooses the silver casket only to find the portrait not of her but of a 'blinking idiot'. By *slapstick*, *caricature* or sheer *ridiculousness of situation*, comedy can be exaggerated into farce, which Shakespeare knows how to use on occasion. At the opposite extreme, before he averts the threat, he can carry it to the brink of tragedy, but always under control.

Dramatic irony is the result of a character or the audience anticipating an outcome which, comically or tragically, turns out very differently. Sometimes *we* foresee that it will. The speaker never foresees how ironical, looking back, the words or expectations will appear. When she says, 'A little water clears us of this deed' Lady Macbeth has no prevision of her sleep-walking words, 'Will these hands ne'er be clean?' There is irony in the way in which in all Shakespeare's tragic plays except *Richard II* comedy is found in the very heart of the tragedy. The Porter scene in *Macbeth* comes straight after Duncan's murder. In *Hamlet* and *Antony and Cleopatra* comic episodes lead into the catastrophe: the rustic Countryman brings Cleopatra the means of death, and the satirised Osric departs with Hamlet's assent to the fatal fencing match. The Porter, the Countryman and Osric are not mere 'comic relief', they contrast with the tragedy in a way that adds something to it, and affects our response.

A sense of the comic and the tragic is common ground between Shakespeare and his audience. Understandings shared with the audience are necessary to all drama. They include conventions, i.e. assumptions, contrary to what factual realism would demand, which the audience silently agrees to accept. It is, after all, by a convention, what Coleridge called a 'willing suspension of disbelief', that an actor is accepted as Hamlet. We should let a play teach us the conventions it depends on. Shakespeare's conventions allow him to take a good many liberties, and he never troubles about inconsistencies that wouldn't trouble an audience. What matters to the dramatist is the effect he creates. So long as we are responding as he would wish, Shakespeare would not care whether we could say by what means he has made us do so. But to appreciate his skill, and get a fuller understanding of his play, we have to distinguish these means, and find terms to describe them.

If you approach the Shakespeare play you are studying bearing in mind what is said to you here, then you will respond to it more fully than before. Yet like all works of artistic genius, Shakespeare's can only be analysed so far. His drama and its poetry will always have about them something 'which into words no critic can digest'.

HAROLD BROOKS

1 WILLIAM SHAKESPEARE
1564 — 1616

1.1 LIFE AND BACKGROUND

Between the record of his christening in 1564 and his burial in 1616, Shakespeare is named in some forty official documents and his family in many more. However, there is little continuous detail of his career, a deficiency which represents a tempting prospect to the biographer with a taste for speculation! Restricting ourselves as far as possible to fact, we may observe that Shakespeare's life fell into three clearly defined stages:

(a) Stratford 1564-87(?)

Baptised on 26 April, William Shakespeare was the third child of his parents, and the first to survive infancy; he was to be followed by five brothers and sisters, only one of whom would outlive him. His mother, Mary Arden, came from a respectable family of local landowners. His father, John, was an honoured citizen of Stratford, at that time a thriving market town with a population of some 1500. John Shakespeare made and sold gloves and other leather goods, as well as dealing in wool, barley and real estate. He held a variety of civic offices, culminating in his election in 1568 as bailiff, or mayor. After 1577, however, he experienced declining fortunes; he stopped attending the council, and in 1580 appears to have been fined, possibly for non-attendance at church.

The young William would have received an orthodox protestant upbringing; religious observance was required by law, as his father knew to his cost. We may assume that Shakespeare attended the local grammar school, where the masters would have provided the traditional fare: an overwhelming concentration on Latin, no mathematics or natural sciences, and precious little reading for pleasure.

It is likely that Shakespeare left school at the age of sixteen. Perhaps he worked for his father or undertook private tutoring. Whatever his occupation, Shakespeare was embarking on his adult life in a Stratford which has been graphically described as a dull and unsavoury place, where the only excitements were provided by christenings, weddings and funerals, the arraignment of citizens for leaving dunghills outside their houses (this had happened to John Shakespeare once), long sermons, takings in adultery, non-attendance at church (John Shakespeare again), witch baiting, the torture of animals, hunting by the gentry, gross and bloody football, the reported appearance of ghosts . . . fairs, itinerant balladmongers' visits, seasonal ceremonies, cows lowing in labour . . . the sticking of swine, flies in summer, frozen pumps in winter, plague, dysentery, fornication . . . drunkenness, threats of damnation from religious fanatics, skittles, poaching, the young beating up the old, harvest home, the re-thatching of roofs, fires raging through dry timber structures, ways foul after rainfall, trees down in storms, coarse jokes, toothache, the scurvy of a bad winter diet. (Anthony Burgess, *Shakespeare*, Jonathan Cape, 1970).

In 1582, Shakespeare married Anne Hathaway. He was eighteen, his bride twenty-six and three months pregnant. Their daughter, Susanna, was born in 1583 and twins, Hamnet and Judith, in 1585. Why did this married man with three children leave Stratford shortly afterwards for a career in London which would keep him from home for a quarter of a century? Burning ambition, or domestic unhappiness? It is idle to speculate, but almost certainly Shakespeare's imagination and intellect were captured by the visiting troupes of actors who performed frequently in Stratford in the 1580s and who did so much to alleviate the dullness of life in a Tudor market town.

(b) London 1587(?)-1611

In London, Shakespeare found a walled city with a population of 200,000: a bustling, cramped and noisy city, a place of dirt and magnificence, with narrow cobbled streets and no drainage, a city dominated by its river, on which might be seen the splendour of royal barges – and the severed heads spiked on London Bridge.

Acting was a precarious way of life and attracted a very mixed response: huge enjoyment from enthusiastic audiences and sour disapproval from the protestant city fathers. This did not prevent frequent performances in a variety of venues, from noblemen's houses to village greens, from local halls to learned colleges; particularly popular were the courtyards of inns, though here the players often had to give way to carts and coaches – and share the profits with the innkeeper! In 1576 the authorities required all companies of actors to be licensed, and provided the actor-manager James Burbage with the incentive to build at Shoreditch, a safe distance outside the city walls, a permanent playhouse which he named 'The Theatre'. The insecurity remained, however, and companies were forced to seek the patronage of the rich and wealthy, even of royalty. When James Burbage built his theatre he was the leader of Leicester's Men; his son, Richard, would be joined by Shakespeare as a prominent member of the Lord Chamberlain's Men. Ben Jonson and Edward Alleyn dominated the Lord Admiral's Men, and the Queen bestowed her patronage on her own company in 1583.

A typical company might include 12-15 principals (who shared the profits), 10-12 extras or hired men, and 3-4 boys for the female roles. There might be a playwright on a small salary, though he would also be called upon to act. Such a playwright would be expected to produce two or three plays per year. The company owned the manuscripts and would be distinctly unenthusiastic about publication; plays were to be watched, not read, and the absence of any effective copyright meant that there was the danger of filching by a rival company. During Shakespeare's life only eighteen of his plays were published, the first eight without his name.

Though we rightly revere the work of Shakespeare, we must constantly remind ourselves that his plays were originally working scripts, no doubt written in haste and freely hacked about and revised in rehearsal and performance. The pressure of work must have been intense, with the plays changed daily and often a total of fifteen or so performed in a month. There was the added demand of mounting special performances, perhaps at a noble residence or even at the court itself.

The audience for a public performance would be extremely varied, ranging from young aristocrats at the edge of the stage – where best to see and be seen – to the lords and ladies in the exclusive accommodation, the merchants in the galleries and the groundlings jostling in the standing enclosure. All with their own tastes and expectations, all needing to be pleased. In no sense did the playhouses enjoy the respectable image of today. Castigated by the authorities on moral grounds, they were also deemed to pose a risk to public health – often being closed at times of plague – and suffered intermittently from riotous behaviour by bands of disaffected apprentices.

Into this volatile context stepped William Shakespeare, to give shape and thrust to the burgeoning of Elizabethan theatre. His early plays were probably written in 1588-90; certainly by 1592 he was sufficiently well-known to attract a scurrilous attack by Robert Greene, who resented Shakespeare's success and lack of scholarly credentials. By 1594, when the playhouses re-opened after a two-year plague closure, Shakespeare was documented as a leading member of the Lord Chamberlain's Men, based at The Theatre. When in 1599 his company moved to the newly-built Globe, Shakespeare was listed as a shareholder. Enhanced status followed in 1603, when James I offered his patronage to the company, which thus became the King's Men. When in 1608 they occupied a roofed theatre at Blackfriars – the venue for Shakespeare's final plays – he was once more established as an important shareholder.

Shakespeare's career in London may be divided into four stages:

(i) *Apprenticeship*: the time of the early plays, up to the plague closure in 1593-4.

4

(ii) *Growing fame*: 1594-9 and the move to the Globe: the established playwright.

(iii) *The tragic phase*: 1599-1608, the period at the Globe in which Shakespeare procuded his great tragedies.

(iv) *The last plays*: 1608-11.

Although the dates of Shakespeare's plays are imprecise, to group them broadly into these four periods and into their varying types allows some insight into the changing pre-occupations of the maturing playwright:

APPRENTICESHIP 1587(?)–94

Comedies	Histories	Tragedies
The Comedy of Errors	*Henry VI Parts*	*Titus Andronicus*
The Taming of the Shrew	*I, II, III*	
The Two Gentlemen of Verona	*Richard III*	
Love's Labour's Lost	*King John*	

GROWING FAME 1594-9

Comedies	Histories	Tragedies
A Midsummer Night's Dream	*Richard II*	*Romeo and Juliet*
The Merchant of Venice	*Henry IV Part I*	
The Merry Wives of Windsor	*Henry IV Part II*	
Much Ado About Nothing	*Henry V*	
As You Like It		

THE TRAGIC PHASE 1599-1608

Comedies	Histories	Tragedies
Twelfth Night		*Julius Caesar*
Troilus and Cressida		*Hamlet*
Measure for Measure		*Othello*
All's Well That Ends Well		*Timon of Athens*
		King Lear (1605)
		Macbeth
		Antony and Cleopatra
		Coriolanus

THE LAST PLAYS 1608-11

Comedies	Histories	Tragedies
Pericles		
Cymbeline		
The Winter's Tale		
The Tempest	*Henry VIII*	

It is evident that in the first half of his career, Shakespeare busied himself with comedy and English history; that he then moved into the sombre period of the great tragedies, a time when even his comic writing was touched by a sardonic shadow or the poignancy of regret; that in his declining years he returned once more to comedy, though a comedy unlike earlier plays – gentle, wise and elegiac, with a harmonising theme of reconciliation and forgiveness.

To what should we attribute the remarkable coherence of Shakespeare's tragic phase? Perhaps the national mood which, after a peak of euphoria following the defeat of the Spanish Armada in 1588, grew restless and uneasy as the century drew to a close. The war with Spain continued, the economy was fragile, but above all there was anxiety about who would succeed Queen Elizabeth – an insecurity hardly soothed by Essex's reckless attempt to seize power in 1601. Even after the accession of James I, the Gunpowder Plot of 1605 – a desperate attempt to assassinate the King and his ministers – bore testimony to continuing instability.

Perhaps the tragic phase was also an expression of something characteristic of Shakespeare's own life at this time. Throughout the 1590s he had gained much: fame, wealth, a coat of arms in 1599, extensive property in Stratford. But now, increasingly, he could also count the losses: his son Hamnet in 1596, his father in 1601, his mother in 1608. Perhaps, as he entered the final third of his life, he could feel the shadows gathering around him.

(c) Stratford 1611–16

When Shakespeare returned to Stratford he was already a wealthy man: a property owner and a major shareholder in two theatres, the Globe and the Blackfriars. Although his days as active company member and playwright were over, at the beginning of this period he completed his final play, *Henry VIII*, and seems to have collaborated with John Fletcher in the writing of *The Two Noble Kinsmen*.

Shakespeare's final choice of role, however, was as a member of Stratford's landed gentry. He had bought New Place in 1597 and enlarged his garden by the purchase of adjacent land; he inherited his father's house in Henley Street and bought a considerable amount of property outside Stratford. Prosperity was assured and no doubt greatly relished. Following his death at the age of 52, William Shakespeare was buried on 23 April 1616 in Holy Trinity Church, Stratford – the church in which he had been christened.

1.2 SOURCES OF KING LEAR

There had certainly been many versions of the Lear story before Shakespeare turned his hand to it. Possibly one of the earliest was in Geoffrey of Monmouth's *Historia Regum Britanniae*, written in the twelfth century.

Edmund Spenser had given a brief treatment of the tale in *The Faerie Queene* (begun in 1579) and perhaps Shakespeare read or saw a production of a play registered in 1594, though not printed until 1605: *The Moste Famouse Chronicle Historye of Leire Kinge of England and his Three Daughters*. In this work Shakespeare would have found a simple and melo-dramatic treatment of the storyline, marked by clumsy humour and a 'happy ending' in which Cordelia is victorious and restores Lear to the throne.

As always with Shakespeare, the source material was transformed and enriched, specifically by the addition of: the sub-plot (borrowed in outline from Philip Sidney's *Arcadia*); the characters of the Fool and, substantially, of Kent; the storm scenes; Lear's madness; the rivalry of Goneril and Regan; the cruel and unexpectedly tragic climax.

1.3 FIRST PERFORMANCE

The first documented performance of *King Lear* was given in the presence of James I on 26 December 1606. An entry in the Stationers' Register on 26 November 1607 refers to the play 'as yt was played before the Kings maiestie at Whitehall vppon St Stephans night at Christmas Last by his maiesties servantes playing usually at the globe on the Banksyde'.

2 SUMMARIES AND
CRITICAL COMMENTARY

2.1 PLOT SUMMARY

Duped by their proclamations of love, Lear divides his kingdom between Goneril and Regan, his elder daughters, and disinherits Cordelia – the youngest and his favourite – for refusing to mouth similar flattery. Lear banishes Kent for supporting Cordelia, and announces that he will live in turn with Goneril and Regan. The King of France takes Cordelia as his wife and they depart. Edmund, Gloucester's bastard son, plans to oust Edgar, his legitimate brother, by persuading Gloucester that Edgar is plotting against him. Meanwhile, Lear has moved in with Goneril, where the disguised Kent joins him as a manservant. Goneril is furious at the wayward behaviour of Lear, his Fool and his knights, and insists that he should dismiss half his retinue. The enraged Lear leaves for Regan's castle.

To avoid Lear, Regan and Cornwall travel to Gloucester's castle, where they arrive just after Edmund has manoeuvred his brother into flight and Gloucester into the delusion that Edgar sought to kill him. Kent thrashes Oswald, Goneril's servant, and is thrown into the stocks by Cornwall. When he arrives, Lear is angered by this insult and by Regan's tardiness in greeting him. Regan is joined by Goneril and they insist that their father must dismiss his entire retinue. The distracted Lear rushes into the night and his daughters lock the doors against him.

Lear, accompanied on the storm-wracked heath by the Fool and Kent, meets Edgar, who is disguised as a bedlam lunatic. Gloucester leads them all to shelter, whereupon the demented Lear 'tries' his cruel daughters. Fearing for his life, Lear's followers convey him to Dover, where French forces are massing to intervene on his behalf. Hearing from the treacherous Edmund of his father's support for Lear, Cornwall gouges out Gloucester's eyes. though he himself is wounded by a horrified servant.

Gloucester, unaware that he is led by Edgar in the guise of a bedlamite, sets out for Dover. Goneril and Edmund, now lovers, hear of Cornwall's death as Albany, horrified by the cruelty of the sisters, determines to help Lear. At Dover, Gloucester 'leaps' in a suicide attempt from an imaginary cliff and, when he 'survives', is persuaded by Edgar that providence has saved him. Lear, crazed still, encounters Gloucester and is then found by Cordelia's search party. The opportunist Oswald attacks Gloucester, but Edgar kills him and discovers Goneril's love letter to Edmund. Cordelia receives the exhausted Lear into her care.

As the sisters compete for Edmund, Edgar passes the incriminating letter to Albany, who is preparing to fight the invaders despite his misgivings. Cordelia's forces are defeated and she and Lear captured. Albany confronts the illicit lovers and sounds a challenge to combat. Edgar, unrecognised in his armour, mortally wounds Edmund and finally reveals his identity, recounting Gloucester's death from a broken heart. A messenger announces that Goneril has poisoned Regan and stabbed herself. Before dying, Edmund reveals that he has ordered the execution of Lear and Cordelia, but the news comes too late. Lear enters, carrying Cordelia's dead body, and then he too dies. Albany calls upon Edgar and Kent to rule with him, but Kent looks forward only to his own death.

2.2 SCENE SUMMARIES AND COMMENTARIES

Act 1, Scene i

Summary

Kent and Gloucester are discussing Lear's plan to sub-divide his kingdom. Gloucester is accompanied by his bastard son, Edmund – the butt of several coarsely jocular remarks by his father. After his ceremonial entry, Lear reveals his intention to divide his kingdom into three and give up the throne. He is accompanied by his three daughters: Goneril and her husband Albany, Regan and her husband Cornwall, and Cordelia – the youngest and Lear's favourite – whose hand is sought by the Duke of Burgundy and the King of France. Lear proclaims that the size of each daughter's share will depend on her declaration of love for him. Goneril and Regan mouth the required flattery. However, Cordelia states that she loves her father no more and no less than duty requires. Lear is enraged and demands that she reconsider. When Cordelia stands firm, he curses and disowns her. Her portion is to be divided between Goneril and Regan. Lear had planned to live with Cordelia, but now will spend alternate months with the two favoured daughters. When Kent attempts to defend Cordelia, he is spurned and finally banished. Burgundy withdraws when he hears that Cordelia is without a dowry, but France takes her as his Queen. Lear and his courtiers quit the stage. In taking leave of her sisters, Cordelia expresses her fears for her father's treatment at their hands. When Goneril and Regan are alone, Cordelia's judgement is borne out, for they speak scathingly of Lear, his rashness and fickleness – and of their need to act together in dealing with him.

Commentary

The first scene introduces all the major characters except Edgar and the Fool, and hinges upon the conflict of wills from which the plot develops.

Kent and Gloucester reveal that this is a time of flux, with the future of the country uncertain (1-7). Their exchange is in *prose* - often reserved by Shakespeare for conversational interludes. It is certainly appropriate for the vulgarity with which Gloucester refers to Edmund (9-24). This taciturn individual is established as a man of ambition, for we hear that he has been seeking his fortune abroad for some nine years (32-33).

No dramatic impact surpasses a processional entry, and the ceremonial arrival of Lear, his daughters and courtiers gains from the juxtaposition with what has been a relatively empty arena. This more stately mood is enhanced by a shift to *verse*. Lear savours his patriarchal performance; the verse of his first speech moves expansively, and the royal plural resounds throughout: 'our darker purpose', 'we have divided', 'our fast intent', 'our age' (37-40). Notice Lear's stress on avoiding 'future strife' (45) - an abiding preoccupation in the Elizabethan mind, with its fear of civil war.

Lear's whim - 'Which of you shall we say doth love us most' (52) - is a show of idle vanity. He has *already* decided on the division; we hear in line 87 that he has prepared 'A third more opulent' for Cordelia. Nonetheless, Goneril understands what is required and turns the situation to her advantage. Her practised flattery points to her character, while 'Dearer than eye-sight' (57) introduces ironically one of the play's major lines of imagery. Regan's 'I am made of that self mettle' (70), with its hint of steel, characterises her hardness of heart as she competes with her sister. Goneril and Regan are putting on a display for an approving Lear and his circle of courtiers. Where is Cordelia? Perhaps somewhat removed from the group, and in her two asides (63 and 77-9) sharing with the audience her own unease and a note of anguished privacy in the midst of ceremonial. Her doubts project her own sincerity and reinforce our distrust of her sisters.

Lear's rewarding of Goneril and Regan reveals his superficial judgement and complacent satisfaction. It is garlanded with the language of bounty: 'rich'd', 'plenteous', 'wide-skirted', 'ample', 'fair', 'space', 'pleasure' (65-82). When he turns to his youngest daughter and hears that Cordelia can offer 'Nothing' (88), the contrast is startling and, like many shocks, it reverberates:

CORDELIA: Nothing, my lord.
LEAR: Nothing?
CORDELIA: Nothing.
LEAR: Nothing will come of nothing: speak again (88-91).

The word is to echo throughout the play.

What are we to make of Cordelia's response, particularly in lines 93-4, where she voices a rather legalistic view of affection? It is certainly, as we see at the end of the scene, a cool understatement of her feelings, into which she has been provoked by Lear's vanity and the hypocritical gush of her sisters. Nevertheless, she knows her father – and his needs – and must to some extent be charged with harshness. Is her inflexibility in part responsible for the gathering crisis?

Lear's rage, when it breaks, is awesome. In his majestic disclaiming of Cordelia, he is intimidatingly a king. The insistent alliteration on 'p' gives rhythmic emphasis to his terrible casting out:

> Here I disclaim all my paternal care,
> Propinquity and property of blood. (114-15)

Notice too that he has been jarred out of his courtly use of the royal plural. The concluding impact of 'Thou my sometime daughter' (121) is withering in its finality. In his defence of Cordelia, we see Kent to be a man of reason and courage. Lear, however, will brook no opposition: the 'Dragon' (123) is not to be challenged.

Lear's rashness accelerates when he shares Cordelia's portion between Goneril and Regan. His flawed judgement is best seen, however, in his intention to retain one hundred knights and 'The name and all th'addition to a king' (134-7). Now he returns to the lofty royal plural, as he ordains the circumstances which are to ruin him. On the one hand he wishes to be relieved of responsibility, while on the other he wishes to retain the trappings of power and status. Thus his vanity prepares the way for disaster, for his knights are to be a key factor in his quarrels with Goneril and Regan.

Kent's final approach to Lear is meant to soothe: 'Royal Lear', 'King', 'father', 'master', 'great patron' (140-3). When this, too, is rejected, his plunge into straight talking is breathtaking:

> . . . be Kent unmannerly
> When Lear is mad. What wouldst thou do, old man? (146-7)

The references to 'mad' and 'old man' force aside the mask of majesty and point forward to the derangement and vulnerability of Lear's desolation.

Kent is the voice of reason. He consolidates our view of Goneril and Regan with his disparaging talk of 'flattery' and 'hollowness' and correctly diagnoses Lear's 'hideous rashness' (149-52). The ability or inability to *see* – to understand oneself and judge others clearly – is a central concern of the play, and is exemplified in the exchange:

> LEAR: Out of my sight!
> KENT: See better, Lear: and let me still remain
>   The true blank of thine eye. (158-60)

When Lear reaches for his sword, Kent challenges him with seeking to punish the doctor and reward 'the foul disease' (164-5). This initiates another significant line of imagery, for references to disease frequently symbolise immoral behaviour. Kent's final charge - 'thou dost evil' (167) - brings a banishment pronounced in the fiercest of terms (168-80). Lear has never previously been so challenged and his pride cannot bear it. His wayward judgement in casting out Cordelia and Kent deprives him of those who genuinely love him, the representatives of reason and true affection. He cannot *see* this, or the fact that he is isolating himself.

Note the rhyming couplets of Kent's farewell (181-8): a technique often used to round off a scene or episode with crisp emphasis. This is to be repeated when Lear (264-8) and Cordelia (281-2) leave the stage. Note also that invocations of the gods (111, 161, 179) do much to establish an early ethos of paganism.

When Burgundy and France appear, Lear's frenzy moves him to a disturbingly bitter outburst against Cordelia (198-206). The theme of Nature, of what is natural and unnatural in behaviour and attitudes, recurs frequently. The idea underpins Lear's dismissal of Cordelia:

> a wretch whom Nature is asham'd
> Almost t'acknowledge hers. (213-14)

The irony, of course, is that it is Lear himself who is behaving unnaturally. Cordelia's final words to her father, with her condemnation of

> that glib and oily art
> To speak and purpose not (225-6)

represent a spirited defence of herself - she is clearly a determined character - and a direct attack on hypocrisy and dissimulation. When Lear and his courtiers have swept off stage, Cordelia challenges her sisters. 'The jewels of our father' (270) picks up the idea of Regan's 'mettle' or 'metal' (70): there is hardness and glitter here, but no feeling. With 'wash'd eyes' and 'profess'd bosoms' (270, 274), she captures the hollowness of their posturing. 'I would prefer him to a better place' (276) establishes an ominous tone, as well as our understanding that in spite of Lear's treatment of her, Cordelia still loves him and bears no grudge. Thus the fineness of her character is emphasised.

As the scene began, so it ends, with two characters in conversation. When Goneril and Regan are alone the dialogue reverts to prose - a fitting medium for the intimacy of their exchanges and for their clinical analysis of their father's changeable moods. It is ironic that they are *right* in their diagnosis; they are identifying his 'tragic flaw', but they do so with no warmth and much scorn. Goneril's dismissal of her father as 'rash' (297) echoes Kent (152), but the latter spoke from concern, while Goneril is moved by disdain. The contrast with their public declarations of love is overwhelming, and fixes them in our minds as hard and ruthlessly self-seeking. Their prediction of trouble ahead (297-302) confirms the mood of foreboding, as does their resolve to act together against their father.

The towering monarch who has dealt out such rough justice is now himself on the brink of vulnerability.

Act I, Scene ii

Summary

A day has passed and the scene is Gloucester's castle. Edmund voices openly his resentment at his status. He pledges himself to a compulsive drive to satisfy his desires, exulting in his bastardy; he is as good as any legitimate son, if not better - more vigorous, more full-blooded. He brandishes a forged letter designed to dispossess Edgar and secure his position for himself. Edmund allows Gloucester an 'accidental' sight of the letter and succeeds in arousing his suspicions. He claims that it was written by Edgar; the letter complains that the young are denied their inheritance for too long, and suggests that Edgar and Edmund should meet to discuss this. Gloucester takes the bait and curses Edgar, whom Edmund pretends to defend, suggesting an arranged test of his loyalty. Gloucester attributes these upheavals to heavenly disturbances - a view scorned by Edmund when the old man has left.

Edgar enters and is as easily trapped as his father. He is bewildered by Edmund's account of Gloucester's wrath and his suggestion that he should hide and arm himself. The scene closes with Edmund's complacent delight at having tricked both his father and his brother.

Commentary

Edmund is much changed from the sombre character of the first scene. Consider his position on stage: he strides to the edge, confronting the audience with his lust for status. He shows a combative vigour, precisely expressed in 'the lusty stealth of nature' (11) and in the belligerent questions which dominate his opening speech and encapsulate his rejection of moral standards. The words 'nature' and 'natural' are picked up again here; for Lear and Gloucester they represent behavioural norms, all that is part of the right order of things. But Edgar, as he inverts accepted standards by exalting bastardy above legitimacy, reverses this also; *his* goddess of Nature presides over the altar of self-interest and scorn for convention. Marriage is 'a dull, stale, tired bed' (13) and legitimate children 'a whole tribe of fops' (14). Edmund's flaunting of the letter and his determination to 'top th'legitimate' (21) evoke our antipathy, but perhaps also a certain fascination at such flagrant self-will.

Gloucester's bewilderment at recent events is seen in the broken verse structure of his anxious musings (23-5). Note the transition to prose for the conversational exchanges - and Edmund's masterly pose as the respectful son. His performance with the letter is compelling: allowing a brief sight to arouse curiosity, feigning unwillingness to reveal the contents, while hinting at their sinisterness, and pretending to defend Edgar, yet blackening his name.

The letter focuses upon a central theme: the transfer of power and wealth from the old to the young. It is re-emphasised in Edgar's alleged view that 'sons at perfect age, and fathers declined, the father should be as ward to the son, and the son manage his revenue' (74-6). The views, of course, are Edmund's, and will find a harsh echo in the mouths of Goneril and Regan.

Gloucester knows neither the handwriting nor the respective worth of his children. In the completeness of his duping he stands condemned, as did his king, of base misjudgement. Note Gloucester's denunciation of Edgar as 'unnatural' (78) in an outburst which recalls the unfettered rage of Lear (77-81). The repeated 'brutish' (78-9) establishes a line of imagery in which despicable behaviour is characterised as animal or sub-human: see this continued in line 97, with 'He cannot be such a monster'. Gloucester's superstitious lament about recent eclipses (107-13) suggests the pagan ethos while also embodying the Elizabethan preoccupation with order, balance, hierarchy, sequence. In 'We have seen the best of our time' (116-17) his mind plays on the fear that Lear's abdication and division of the kingdom are part of a disturbance of the natural equilibrium.

After the exit of Gloucester, Edmund's philosophy is again projected in his scathing dismissal of his father's beliefs. For him, the stars have no significance; man is what he makes himself, no more, no less. This adds point, of course, to his cynical aping of his father in 148-54, after the entry of Edgar. Note the emphasis given to his mock solemnity by the thudding alliteration on 'd': 'death', 'dearth', 'dissolutions', 'divisions', 'diffidences', 'dissipation' (150-3). This litany of disruption is precisely what Edmund aspires to achieve.

Edgar's character is established by his affectionate greeting of Edmund, who sets about manipulating him as he did his father. Is Edgar naive or simply too noble to harbour suspicions? We see too little here to come to any conclusions, but when he has been sent packing, our view of Edmund is confirmed. He rounds off the scene with the same vaunting cynicism as he began, reverting to verse and concluding with an emphatic couplet (185-90). He exults in his disdain for those closest to him - 'A credulous father and a brother noble' (185) - and derides Edgar's 'foolish honesty' (187). Ideals are spurned as he proclaims his doctrine of the end justifying the means: 'All with me's meet that I can fashion fit' (190). Here is a man indubitably evil, ruthlessly selfish and deceitful. Should one also register an intimidated regard for the energy of his ambition, his skill and sardonic humour?

Thus another family is disrupted. However, whereas Lear dislocated the harmony of his family in a tempestuous passion, Edmund coolly plans for it.

The structural significance of this scene is that it initiates the sub-plot, which reveals several parallels with the main action:
(a) the gulling of a credulous parent;
(b) an innocent child abused;
(c) deluded regard for base and selfish offspring.

Act 1, Scene iii

Summary
We are in the palace of the Duke of Albany, where Goneril is receiving an account of Lear's riotous behaviour. She will refuse to speak to her father, and instructs Oswald to be disrespectful to him. If he should object, he may go to Regan, although Goneril is confident that her sister would act similarly. In any event, she will write to Regan to propose a common approach.

Commentary
For the first time we hear of the Fool (1-2), and his partial responsibility for provoking the troubles which are to engulf his master.
    Goneril is now the enraged *grande dame*. Imagine her bustling on to the stage with Oswald in her wake, seething with accumulated grievance (3-5). Her fears about Lear's rashness have been borne out. We receive an intriguing picture of a wildly impetuous Lear, even now out hunting; we are eager to see this erratic and wilful king. There is some justification in

> Idle old man,
> That still would manage those authorities
> That he hath given away! (17-19)

Lear *has*, it would seem, been unable to shake off his imperious manner. Again we reflect on the uneasy transfer of power from old to young. What removes any sympathy for Goneril is her dismissive scorn for 'old fools' (20), and the fact that she seeks to manufacture a confrontation. In this, as well as in writing to Regan, she is beginning to plot against Lear, and we are irredeemably alienated.

Act I, Scene iv

Summary
Kent proposes to serve Lear under cover of disguise. On his return from hunting, the arrogant Lear is taken aback by the planned insolence. Having questioned Kent, he engages his services immediately when he trips Oswald. The Fool, whom we meet for the first time, repeatedly jibes at Lear's stupidity.
    When Lear challenges Goneril about her coldness, her reply is a torrent

of resentment at the behaviour of Lear's followers. Against a chorus of acerbic comments from the Fool, Lear's first response is angered bewilderment. Goneril, not to be diverted, demands a reduction in his retinue and Lear now gives way to rage. He perceives the pettiness of Cordelia's 'offence' and begins to realise his misguided action. Albany, shaken by the clash, protests his innocence as Lear delivers a terrible curse on his daughter. Hearing that his retinue is to be halved, Lear is reduced to weeping – and to the desperate hope of consolation from Regan. The sympathetic Albany is treated with contempt by his wife, who despatches a letter to Regan informing her of Lear's behaviour.

Commentary

After the sinister overtones of the preceding scenes, it is a relief to see a reassertion of goodness and loyalty in Kent's determination to serve Lear. Lear, however, makes a raucous entry, and his peremptory curtness (9) confirms that Goneril may have cause for complaint. Kent's creed of honesty (14-18) highlights recent hypocrisy, and his observation that he is 'as poor as the king' (20-1) provokes the first of Lear's cries of self-pity (22-3).

Note the mannerly words and discreet concern of Lear's knight (51, 54-5, 57-62, 64-6 and 73-4), who is one of the retinue resented by Goneril. Should we visualise them in *her* terms as coarse and licentious or, as Lear is to defend them, 'men of choice and rarest parts' (265)? In describing 'a great abatement of kindness' towards Lear, the knight is identifying the first stage of his isolation, while in commenting on the Fool's pining for Cordelia, he allows a glimpse of the king's anguished sensitivity (75-6).

Consider Lear's 'Who am I, sir?' (78). At this point, the question represents an angered insistence on status. Oswald's pert reply (79) is the first overt denial of Lear's majesty, and we share in what must have been the groundlings' delight when Lear cuffs him and Kent applies the *coup de grace*.

The Fool is more a device than a rounded character. Concentrate on visualising his stage presence and function: spry, nimble-footed, for ever at Lear's elbow (or behind him), dancing attendance while holding up an unforgiving mirror to his folly. Although devoted to his master, the Fool spares Lear not at all; he is constantly probing the tender spot, forcing him to confront the enormity of his error. Within minutes he has dubbed Kent a fool for wishing to serve Lear (97-104); offered the same taunt to Lear for giving everything to his daughters (105-10); charged him with favouring lies (112-14); saluted the virtues of discretion which Lear has lacked (119-28); developed, crucially, the *leitmotif* of the 'nothing' into which Lear is to be plunged (129-36, 187-8, 193-7); and identified the inversion of natural order which Lear has fostered (160-3, 172-4, 225).

Does the Fool relish his task because he cannot forgive the casting out of Cordelia? Perhaps, but one should not understate the closeness between servant and master, an intimacy exemplified in their mutual use of such 'pet' names as 'nuncle', 'boy', 'lad'. Lear's response to the Fool is complex, veering between kindly indulgence and pained threats of a whipping (111, 181). It is this complexity which begins to flesh out Lear in our imaginations and to engage, possibly for the first time, our sympathy.

This developing view of Lear as victim is consolidated by the Fool's return to the insistent negative – 'I am a fool, thou art nothing' (194–5) – and by the harshness of Goneril's attack (202–15). Notice her distant use of 'sir' (202) and that for the icy anger of her protest we return to verse. Her onslaught strikes Lear momentarily dumb, but brings a chilling comment from the Fool:

> The hedge-sparrow fed the cuckoo so long
> That it's had it head bit off by it young. (217–18)

The pattern of ferocious animal imagery is continued, as is the theme of the old brutally dispossessed by the young.

The 'identity question' identified in line 78 now finds a reverberation in the bewildered 'Are you our daughter?' (220), soon to be followed by the sarcastic 'Your name, fair gentlewoman?' Consider these 'interrogatives of selfhood' in the seminal speech beginning:

> Does any here know me? This is not Lear . . .

and ending:

> Who is it that can tell me who I am? (227–31)

It may be true that Lear is engaging in caustic play-acting to conceal his distress, but we are witnessing also the beginning of an agonised crisis of identity in which he cannot credit that such humiliations can be visited upon *him*. Dismissed as 'My lady's father' (79) by Oswald, the Fool's observation that he is 'Lear's shadow' (232) continues the process of reduction. In demanding 'Where are his eyes?' (228) Lear simply wonders whether he can believe what he sees happening before him; more poignantly his question links with the image pattern in which failing to see physically betokens lack of moral insight.

Goneril's speech of complaint (238–53) stresses again his advanced age and the limitations which she now considers appropriate. Note that she does not cast him out; she offers the option of a reduced retinue. Either she *is* being reasonable, or she knows well what her father's response will be, and is therefore engaging in a cynical gambit.

Lear's outburst, with the fearful connotations of 'Darkness and devils' (254) and the vicious consonants of 'Degenerate bastard' (256), is genuinely disturbing. There is pathos in the self-consolation of 'Yet have I left a daughter' (257), for his certainty must be set alongside *our* more realistic expectations. Where are his eyes, indeed? The verse structure begins to fragment under the pressure of Lear's passion (254-7, 259-63). See how he brokenly bemoans the ingratitude of the young in 261-3 and 290-1. Note that sub-human imagery – 'sea-monster' (263) and 'Detested kite' (264) – defines again the basest of behaviour. Above all, observe that Lear now appreciates the triviality of Cordelia's 'offence' and his own foolishness in treating her as he did (268-74). This is his first step towards self-knowledge.

Why does Lear dismiss Kent and his knights? Is he ashamed of his open distress or does he seek greater privacy for his appalling curse on Goneril (276-91)? The 'Nature' on whom he calls is the benevolent power of fruitfulness. And what he calls down on Goneril, a barren womb and broken heart, is startling in its loathing. Note that he reviles her as an animal: she is a 'creature' (279) who would 'teem' (283). See how this imagery culminates in:

> How sharper than a serpent's tooth it is
> To have a thankless child. (290-1)

Lear's sobs (300-6) are a measure of his catastrophic decline from imperious majesty, and his 'father's curse' (302) verges on the incoherent – the pathetic threats of a little boy confronting an indomitable power. In threatening to pluck out his eyes, we have a terrible foreshadowing of the physical reality which will scar Gloucester's face, and a further hint at the lack of insight which sends Lear in search of comfort from Regan.

This is the first of the great scenes and does much to clarify our view of the characters. For all his waywardness and the vileness of his curses, we *do* sympathise with Lear: partly because the spectacle of such distress is inevitably moving, partly because he is now seeing his past mistake, and partly because Goneril is so unmoved by it all. See how she slaps her husband down (293-5, 315) and dismisses his concern as weakness (342-6), inverting normal values by scorning 'milky gentleness' (343) and 'harmful mildness' (346). She is brisk and business-like at the end of this passionate scene. Thus, we warm to Albany and are further repelled by his flint-hearted wife.

Act I, Scene v

Summary
Kent's first mission is to deliver to Regan a letter announcing her father's forthcoming arrival. The Fool taunts his master about the futility of expecting better treatment from Regan. Lear, however, is preoccupied with other thoughts. Ominously, he fears losing his reason, and prays that he may be spared this. Master and Fool take horse for the journey to Gloucester.

18

Commentary

Lear speaks tenderly to the Fool, laughing helpfully at his prattle; perhaps he is relieved to be quit of Goneril, perhaps warmed by the anticipation of kindness from Regan. More likely, he is not listening to the Fool, who continues to harp on his master's foolishness. 'I did her wrong' (25), isolated in a sea of babble, points up Lear's growing awareness of having offended against Cordelia. He reflects naively on taking up arms (40), but chiefly he is haunted by 'Monster ingratitude' towards 'so kind a father' (33). His fear of madness – the word tolls three times in two lines (46–7) – has a dual effect: it emphasises the scale of present suffering and, in anticipating what is to come, offers a further dimension of pain, for no torment is as great as one which can be foreseen but not avoided.

The very fact of moving outside is the beginning of a growing momentum towards vulnerability, insecurity and exposure.

Act II, Scene i

Summary

It is night and the scene is Gloucester's castle. Edmund hears that Regan and Cornwall are due to arrive and that war is likely between Cornwall and Albany. Edmund determines to turn this to his advantage. He warns Edgar that his refuge has been discovered and questions him about alleged involvement in the quarrels between Cornwall and Albany. Edgar is hounded into flight. Before the arrival of Gloucester, Edmund wounds himself and then convinces the old man that he was hurt by Edgar when he refused to join in a plot against him. Gloucester pledges death for Edgar and promises that Edmund will inherit in his place. On his arrival, Cornwall confirms the death sentence and takes Edmund into his service. Regan explains to Gloucester that she thought it best not to be at home to receive her father and his 'riotous knights'.

Commentary

Consider the symmetry of flight: Lear fleeing in search of comfort from Regan, while she and Cornwall are fleeing to avoid him.

The Elizabethans would have expected dissension between Albany and Cornwall; what else could follow from abdication and division of the realm? The stress is on transition, insecurity, shifting alignments.

Edmund displays the fullness of his wicked talents here, weaving unexpected developments into his plans and acting without hesitation. We witness another superlative performance as he packs his bemused brother from the stage. Examine the turbulent sentence structure of 21–33; Edgar is swamped by questions, statements, warnings, commands. He manages only one sentence of protestation: a pawn indeed.

Edmund's determination is well evidenced in his drawing of his own blood. See the supreme hypocrisy of his describing Edgar's alleged purpose as 'unnatural' (50) and how he claims to have defended the very links which he defiles (47-8). Again the love and trust between a father and a dutiful child are soured. Gloucester – where are *his* eyes? – is profoundly deceived as Edgar joins Cordelia and Kent as another innocent fugitive. The scale of his delusion is seen when Edmund is saluted as 'Loyal and natural boy' (84) and Edgar dismissed with 'I never got him' (78).

Regan and Cornwall arrive with expressions of elaborate concern, but compare their loftiness with the broken grief of Gloucester:

> O! Madam, my old heart is crack'd, it's crack'd. (90)

Their sympathy rings hollow when one considers that they have quit their own home so as to avoid offering comfort to Lear. Note that 'crack'd' is part of an image pattern of breaking, crumbling, shattering which characterises the play and gives depth to the theme of the sundering of kingdoms and families.

Consider how well Goneril has poisoned her sister's mind against her father (94-5, 98-100). See how swift Edmund is to ally himself with the visitors (97). Prepare to wince as Cornwall proclaims Edmund's 'child-like office' (106) and nature 'of such deep trust' (115).

Structurally, this is a most important scene. Edmund takes his first step in self-advancement by usurping his brother's place, and links the sub-plot and main plot by joining Cornwall. We know little about the latter, but we note his willingness to avoid offering solace to Lear and his readiness to promise the execution of Edgar (110-11). Edmund is in suitable company. The grouping of characters further clarifies when we hear that Edgar is the godson of Lear. The evil faction numbers Goneril, Regan, Edmund and Cornwall. As for those enlisting to some extent our sympathy, with Lear and Gloucester deluded, Cordelia, Kent and Edgar banished and Albany a helpless onlooker, there is no doubt that the forces of darkness are in the ascendancy.

Act II, Scene ii

Summary
It is early morning outside Gloucester's castle, where Kent and Oswald await Regan's reply to their letters. In revenge for his impertinence to Lear, Kent abuses and beats Oswald, who does not recognise him. The brawl is halted by Cornwall, although Kent persists in haranguing Oswald and extends his insults to the rest of the party. Feeling his own dignity abused, Cornwall decides to clap Kent into the stocks. Kent protests against this implied insult to Lear: a sentiment supported by Gloucester, who fears the king's reaction. Cornwall is unmoved and Gloucester remains behind to express sympathy for Kent's plight. Left alone, Kent produces a letter from Cordelia, who has learned of the situation and appears to propose some intervention.

Commentary

The early stages provide important comic relief – important because our emotional response requires a respite if it is not to be over-exploited; because, by juxtaposition, the comic interlude lends emphasis to the darker episodes; and because, as Shakespeare understood, the less refined members of his audience would rejoice at the opportunity for a belly laugh. And how they would laugh at the magnificent vigour with which Kent berates Oswald, particularly at his threat to 'daub the wall of a jakes with him' (66-7).

However, we should not underestimate the serious significance. This episode partially rights the balance, strikes a blow (figuratively and literally) for those with whom we sympathise. It shows the current antagonism (Lear/Goneril) enacted by their servants at a lower level. See Kent's splendid reassertion of values when he damns Goneril as 'vanity the puppet' alongside 'the royalty of her father' (35-6), and how he excoriates Oswald as an exponent of the hypocrisy which seeks its own ends and betrays profoundly important bonds:

> Such smiling rogues as these,
> Like rats, oft bite the holy cords a-twain
> Which are too intrince t'unloose. (72-4)

Kent's insulting of Regan and Cornwall (91-4) pleases us enormously, as does his mocking display of the sycophancy which his lordship clearly prefers (104-7).

This is the scene which first gives us the measure of Cornwall; in supporting Oswald, cheaply insulting Kent's age (125) and clapping him in the stocks with no thought for Lear, he first engages our hostility. See also how he brushes aside (145) the anxious protests of Gloucester, whose hospitality he has requisitioned. We recognise the truth of Gloucester's later estimation of Cornwall's temperament (150-2). Regan, whose lack of feminine softness is illustrated by her wish to redouble Kent's punishment (133), is more than well matched.

Events here help to restore Gloucester in our estimation. His coarse banter in the opening scene and his gulling by Edmund have done little to win him our regard. Now we are warmed by his sympathy for Kent (150) and by his interceding with Cornwall (138-45). His repeated warnings that Lear will consider himself insulted (143, 157) establish audience anticipation of his likely response as he travels towards further humiliation.

The letter from Cordelia is a somewhat artificial device, but it serves two important purposes: (a) it re-activates Cordelia as a character; and (b) it balances against the vision of Kent in the stocks – a symbol of Lear's decline – the prospect of support for the king from elsewhere. This hope, distant but real, lingers in the mind as a possibility of salvation throughout the agonies that lie ahead.

Act II, Scene iii

Summary
The scene is a wood. Edgar has eluded arrest by hiding in the hollow of a tree. He decides that the only recourse is to disguise himself; he will cast off his identity and pose as a Bedlam beggar, a wandering madman.

Commentary
This scene conveys urgency and gives some impression of Kent's time in the stocks. It also represents the first real speech from Edgar, who hitherto has simply been manipulated. Now, at last, he acts. The nature of his plight and the forthrightness of his revelation engage the sympathy of the audience. He explains his intention to disguise himself as Kent did at the opening of I.iv. Remember that an audience's involvement is enhanced by being 'in the know' about disguises; there is the appreciation of ironies and double meanings in many contexts, as well as the satisfaction of being aware of facts and situations hidden from some of the characters.

Why a Bedlam lunatic? Because the extremeness, the filth, the demented rantings offer the best chance of escaping detection. The underlying significance is that Edgar's presence in a wood, his talk of vulnerability and exposure, lodge in our minds an image of the bleak and comfortless out-of-doors into which Lear is to be thrust; and his assumed role as Poor Tom prepares us for the actual derangement of Lear. Notice that the final words echo the theme of 'nothing', the annihilation of selfhood. For Edgar, this represents an escape route; for Lear, it will be part of a harrowing process of self-discovery.

Act II, Scene iv

Summary
The scene is Gloucester's castle later in the same day, where Lear is affronted at finding Kent in the stocks. Kent recounts Regan's reaction to Lear's letter and his manhandling of Oswald. Lear goes in search of 'this daughter' and re-enters in a fury when she and Cornwall refuse to see him. When they eventually do appear and free Kent, Lear promptly forgets his servant and craves sympathy. Regan loses no time in defending her sister's stand and suggests that he return with an apology and a smaller retinue. Lear is outraged at the thought and falls into incoherent cursing of Goneril.

Goneril's arrival drives him to distracted rage, but the sisters combine against their father and Regan again suggests that he should return with Goneril. Lear disavows her as a diseased corruption, but when he looks to the consolation of staying with his knights under Regan's roof, she soon disabuses him. She will not accept even fifty knights. Lear recalls emotionally his generosity to them as his daughters finally unite in denying that he needs any followers at all. Lear is broken on the rock of their hardness. As a storm gathers, he stumbles from the stage, terrified anew at the prospect of madness. Regan, Goneril and Cornwall grudgingly concur that Lear may be given shelter, but not a single follower. When Gloucester warns that the old man is preparing to leave, their callous response is to let him go. They withdraw to the shelter of the castle, leaving Lear exposed to the darkness of the night and the wildness of the storm.

Commentary

Lear's first concern is not for Kent, but for the implied insult to himself (11-12, 24, 27). The Fool projects a cynical view of parent/child relationships: the young seek money and inheritance; poor fathers – as Lear now is – can expect only indifference (47-52). Lear is almost choked by the passions welling up inside him. Perhaps shame is why he wishes to confront Regan alone.

Although the Fool again touches on the stupidity of following a waning star, his characterisation gains depth from his expression of loyalty (81-2). This is something of a relief, for he is in danger of being seen as little more than a dispenser of barbed phrases.

As Lear rages impotently, the measure of his decline may be seen in Gloucester's reference to Cornwall's temper; he fears this more than the outbursts of Lear. The monarch who spoke loftily of 'our fast intent' now veers from one extreme to the other: from fierce expostulations to submissiveness as he seeks excuses for their calculated insult (103-10), then to rage at the denial of 'my state' (110). Majesty has been supplanted by the conflicting emotions of a disorientated old man.

Examine the meeting of Lear with Regan and Cornwall. Compare the cold courtesy of their greeting with his eagerness to plead his case:

> Beloved Regan,
> Thy sister's naught: O Regan! she hath tied
> Sharp-tooth'd unkindness, like a vulture, here. (131-3)

How appropriate is the image of a bird of prey, for the sisters are soon to pick his bones clean! Judge Lear's obsessiveness by the ease with which he forgets Kent. Consider the poignancy of our response, for we know that his hopes in Regan are ill-founded.

Lear is a supplicant, beseeching Regan, plucking at her sleeve, watching for a sign of sympathy, and finding none. Perhaps it is seeing her face closed against him that brings his final broken plea:

> I scarce can speak to thee; thou'lt not believe
> With how deprav'd a quality – O Regan! (134-5)

Her rebuttal is chilling; notice her use of 'sir' rather than 'father' and her measured defence of Goneril (140-3). Consider in particular the withering dismissiveness with which she denies the dignity of his great age (144-8). There is some truth in her assertions, but her harshness is clear. Lear can only lampoon with sarcastic self-abasement the suggestion that he should return to Goneril:

> Dear daughter, I confess that I am old;
> Age is unnecessary: on my knees I beg
> That you'll vouchsafe me raiment, bed and food! (152-4)

His caricature is uncomfortably close to the actual views of his daughters.

Lear's self-control collapses in incoherent curses against the 'serpent-like' Goneril (159). The exposure of the heath is foreshadowed in 'You taking airs' (162), 'You nimble lightnings' (163), 'You fen-suck'd fogs' (165). 'Infect her beauty' (164) and 'blister her' (166) measure the fullness of his loathing and reinforce the imagery of disease. His proclamation of Regan's devotion (168-79) is an attempt to reassure himself as she stands coldly surveying him. She will, of course, supply his simple needs:

> The offices of nature, bond of childhood,
> Effects of courtesy, dues of gratitude. (176-7)

She would never — a disturbing irony in view of what is to come —

>   oppose the bolt
> Against my coming in.   (174-5)

Briskly, she deflects his pleas:

> Good sir, to th'purpose. (179)

With the arrival of Goneril, Lear is hemmed in — a quarry indeed. How well they have debased him, for now when he calls out for the intervention of supernatural powers, it is not on behalf of a king, but of a broken old man (188-90). Swiftly they deny him the desired reverence: Goneril dismisses his age as 'dotage' (195), Cornwall admits that he stocked Kent (197-8) and Regan twists the knife: 'I pray you, father, being weak, seem so' (199). He must, she suggests, learn to know his place, and return with Goneril.

Lear is forced into a brief rallying cry of defiance — a marvellous three-stage assertion of pride (205-15), each stage echoing with the horror of 'Return with her?'. Yet even as he takes a stand, his speech foreshadows the imminence of his exclusion:

> No, rather I abjure all roofs, and choose
> To wage against the enmity o'th'air. (206-7)

In the wake of such passion, Lear is pierced by the cold brevity of Goneril's 'At your choice, Sir' (215) and senses again the imminence of madness

(216). Derangement seems close in his tormented effort to bid farewell to Goneril, with its rapid mood changes (216-29).

We are at first moved by 'my child', 'my flesh', 'my blood', 'my daughter'; then jarred by his sudden lurch into hatred –

> Or rather a disease that's in my flesh,
> Which I must needs call mine (220-1) –

then calmed anew by the meekness of 'I'll not chide thee' (223) and the painful naivety of his trust in Regan's hospitality.

Regan's laconic 'Not altogether so' (229) opens a concerted attack in which she and Goneril harry their father and strip him of his retinue (235-61). Imagine him, turning from one to the other, as they warm to their task, saluting him as 'my Lord', offering reasonable explanations . . . and knowing all the time that it is not a matter of soldiers, but of pride. Lear's broken plea, 'I gave you all', draws from Regan the tart rejoinder: 'And in good time you gave it' (248). The theme of usurping youth is reasserted.

We squirm with Lear as he turns to the detested Goneril, revaluing her allowance of fifty knights (254-8), still measuring love in material terms. So far has he fallen, but now the momentum is irresistible and Regan supplies the final thrust: 'What need one?' (261).

Trapped between them, Lear's cry of grief beginning 'O! reason not the need' (262-84) traces in microcosm the pattern of his breakdown. Beginning in lucidity with observations on human need and identity (262-8), he slumps into broken recognition of his plight, a king no longer:

> You see me here, you Gods, a poor old man,
> As full of grief as age; wretched in both! (270-1)

Having begged for patience (269), he now prays for 'noble anger' (274); he desperately wants to be mighty, but can only weep even as he denies it. Now disabused of any lingering hope in his daughters, 'you unnatural hags' (276) represents his first attack on them both. Like a tearful child, he threatens to take revenge, but is not sure how. As he denies again the tears that scald his eyes, the first rumblings of the storm symbolise the tempest within. Thus is his suffering projected on a more than human scale. We note the recurring image of shattering in

> . . . this heart
> Shall break into a hundred thousand flaws (282-3)

and tremble with him that this breaking – certainly, now – will include his mind:

> O Fool! I shall go mad. (284)

The Fool, Gloucester and Kent have been with Lear throughout his agony, but silent, awed by the scale of his anguish.

As for Regan and Goneril, no doubt they have stood aloof as the old man has crumpled before them, poised in their impenetrable cruelty. Their maliciousness is now seen in high relief. The vindictiveness of Goneril allows no sympathy:

> 'Tis his own blame; hath put himself from rest,
> And must needs taste his folly. (288-9)

Gloucester's anxious warning that Lear is preparing to leave gives Goneril scope for further venom:

> My Lord, entreat him by no means to stay. (297)

When Gloucester pleads the coldness of the night and the vast emptiness of the countryside (298-300), Regan commands 'Shut up your doors' (302). We remember with a shudder Lear's confidence that she would never oppose the bolt against him.

Cornwall's final words heighten the foreboding, and the four-fold rhythm of his closing lines seems to echo the sliding of the bolts:

> Shut up your doors, my Lord; 'tis a wild night.
> My Regan counsels well. Come out o'th'storm. (306-7)

Act III, Scene i

Summary
On the heath, Kent meets one of Lear's followers who informs him that the King is defying the storm to do its worst, calling down destruction on a world which has pained him. His only companion is the Fool, who seeks to relieve Lear's anguish by jesting. Kent reveals the enmity between Albany and Cornwall and that civil war is likely. Spies have conveyed this information to Cordelia and French armies have already landed. Kent bids the gentleman make his way to Dover, to report to Cordelia on the sufferings of Lear.

Commentary
This scene performs several important functions. The first is to represent the passage of time, during which we may imagine Lear having journeyed into the wilderness. The second is to create the background of a storm. Shakespeare's plays were first produced in daylight and there were virtually no technical effects. The players had to *act* the storm. Imagine them, fumbling their way along: bent, cowed, shielding their faces, peering heavenwards in hope of abatement. The diction of the opening lines reverberates with the violence of the tempest: 'foul weather', 'unquietly',

'contending', 'fretful elements', 'tears', 'impetuous blasts', 'eyeless rage', 'fury', 'out-storm', 'conflicting wind and rain' (1-11).

Another function is to prepare us for the demented rantings of Lear, which might appear too sudden without a prelude such as this – and might have provoked sniggers from an Elizabethan audience accustomed to mocking mental disturbance.

In Lear's reported defiance, we sense an exalting of the king, a deranged mightiness; yet we see also the fragility of age – the 'white hair' of an 'unbonneted' old man exposed to a night which drives even the fiercest of beasts to shelter (4-15).

Note that the evil faction faces its first set-backs: rivalry between Albany and Cornwall and a French force already landed. Thus is the impetus of evil checked; help, if not at hand, is at least a possibility to be cherished during the torment of 'the old kind king' (28). Dover, mentioned here for the first time, is established as a recurrent symbol of new hope, redemption and reassertion of justice – the port after a storm to which all roads will lead. Before we join Lear in his agony, the seeds of regeneration are already sown.

Act III, Scene ii

Summary

Lear rages against the elements while the Fool veers between jesting and pleas for shelter. Kent stumbles upon his master and begs him to seek refuge, but Lear, who does not recognise Kent, launches a tirade against evil and hypocrisy. Suddenly pierced by an awareness of imminent madness, Lear looks with tender sympathy on the bedraggled Fool and they go in search of the hovel.

Commentary

There is a stark contrast here with the broken old man who stumbled from the stage at the end of Act II. Now Lear has a frenzied grandeur which arises partly from the extremeness of his situation, and the rage with which he confronts it, and partly from the violent verbs that characterise his opening speech: 'blow', 'crack', 'rage', 'spout', 'drench'd', 'drown'd', 'cleaving', 'shaking', 'strike', 'crack', 'spill'. The words and images must be seen as well as heard: visualise churches under water, oaks cracked open, the searing of a frail and aged head, the pillaging of nature's seed-store (1-9). Such is Lear's loathing of a world which has racked him, although we should note that while his passion for annihilation is universal, there is no doubting the *personal* anguish of 'ingrateful man' (9).

This personal pain continues in lines 14-24 as the tone modulates into the pathos of an old man's reproaches:

> I tax not you, you elements, with unkindness;
> I never gave you kingdom, called you children;
> You owe me no subscription. (16-18)

The rhythm slows into a miserable acknowledgement of debasement –

> here I stand, your slave,
> A poor, infirm, weak and despis'd old man (19-20) –

only to quicken into a denunciation of the elements as allies of the exe-
crated daughters (21-4). Lear repeatedly symbolises his vulnerability by
the image of the white head (6, 23-4) – more fragile in the absence of a
crown? Kent himself will take up the theme in 'Alack! bare-headed!'
(60).

The Fool receives scant attention from the preoccupied Lear, who
finds a sudden calm in:

> No, I will be the pattern of all patience;
> I will say nothing. (37-8)

Kent's speech (42-9) may be regarded both as an expression of sympathy and a dramatic device for reasserting the wildness of the night; our
imaginative grasp of the storm must constantly be prompted.

If Lear's sufferings are part of his journey towards awareness, then
the magnificent lines 49-60 represent a landmark. He has already achieved
some insight in acknowledging his wronging of Cordelia and his fragility
as an old man. Now he is possessed of a new vision; the storm is the
instrument of the gods in seeking out and punishing rampant evil, the evil
of hidden guilt and hypocrisy, the evil of Goneril and Regan. The cruelty
to which he has been exposed has opened his eyes to a foul reality which
he never suspected as king. This speech develops a powerful momentum
with its sequence of injunctions to evil-doers, culminating in an honest
assessment of his own guilt:

> I am a man
> More sinn'd against than sinning. (59-60)

There is no self-pity, no self-delusion here; Lear knows he has done wrong,
but rightly judges himself more victim than sinner – further insight in
the midst of derangement.

The anger is spent. Mighty imprecations and furious challenges give
way to gentle stoicism and whispered closeness. Notice Lear's soothing
use of pet names to the Fool – 'my boy', 'my fellow', 'Poor Fool and knave'
(68-73) – and his first expression of sympathy for somebody other than
himself:

> I have one part in my heart
> That's sorry yet for thee. (72-3)

In coaxing the Fool to seek refuge, Lear finds unexpected comfort in the prospect of straw on a mud floor:

> The art of our necessities is strange,
> And can make vile things precious. (70-1)

This is profound insight into the nature of real need, from a man who not long ago judged it in terms of status symbols and material goods. Truly, he is learning, although, ironically, only when he is on the verge of madness.

The Fool's closing lines may be considered a spurious addition. Would Lear be likely to leave him behind after his gentle words of concern?

Act III, Scene iii

Summary
Gloucester reveals to Edmund his distress at the cruelty of Goneril, Regan and Cornwall. He is disturbed at their command that he, the master of the house, should not comfort the King. Confiding in Edmund, he refers to a letter promising armed support for Lear. He urges loyalty to the King, and instructs Edmund to occupy Cornwall so that he may not be discovered in an act of kindness to Lear. Left alone, Edmund determines to disclose to Cornwall his father's sympathies, and the possession of the letter. Thus he anticipates disgracing Gloucester and winning the earldom for himself.

Commentary
This scene represents a quiet interlude which emphasises by contrast the frenzy on either side. We writhe as Gloucester commits his fatal error; nowhere is he more 'blind' than here, although our sympathy is secured by his commitment to Lear. Consider how the ruthlessness of Regan and Cornwall is intensifying, in Gloucester's account of their drive to isolate and crush Lear (2-6) - *'unnatural* dealing', indeed. Note the mockingly ironic repetition by Edmund (7).

Gloucester's determination to serve Lear is balanced by Edmund's determination to serve himself; observe the dreadful irony of the anxious father beseeching the vile son to look after himself. The theme of age thrust out by youth is encapsulated in Edmund's laconic observation:

> The younger rises when the old doth fall. (25)

Goneril and Regan would applaud the sentiment of a kindred spirit.

Main and sub-plots are intertwining as Gloucester draws closer to Lear, and Edmund seeks further favour from Cornwall.

Act III, Scene iv

Summary
To Kent's promptings that he must enter the hovel, Lear replies that his discomfort in the storm is nothing compared to the distress caused by filial ingratitude. Once more he is aware of approaching madness. He ushers the Fool in first, expressing his sympathy for the poor. The Fool runs in terror from the hovel, startled by Poor Tom (Edgar), who is sheltering there. Lear can only believe that the naked beggar has been reduced to this state by cruel daughters. Fascinated by Tom, he interrogates him on his past. His nakedness defines humanity at its most fundamental; Lear seeks to identify with this by tearing off his own clothes.

Gloucester reveals that he has prepared a refuge in a castle outhouse. Lear, however, will not be separated from Tom, a 'philosopher' who has taught him much. The scene ends as the group moves off to shelter, with Lear dancing attendance on his beggar.

Commentary
The callousness of Edmund is succeeded by the anxious concern of Kent. While Lear remains vulnerable - 'Wilt break my heart?' (4) - we see also a continuation of the reflective Lear who pondered on 'The art of our necessities'. He instructs Kent in the relativity of despair: great sorrows cancel out small ones, mighty anguish numbs the mind to physical pain:

> When the mind's free
> The body's delicate. (11-12)

There is the precise evaluation and condensed expression of a moralist in this aphorism.

Yet the violent swings of mood reappear. Lear understands that the storm is within him as well as without (12). The moralist yields to the enraged father. The disturbing image of the mouth tearing the hand that feeds it (15-16) captures the violence of his passion. Examine the broken line structure (16-22) as he veers between threats of vengeance, self-pity and fear of madness.

Just as suddenly, his mood softens into solicitousness:

> Prithee, go in thyself: seek thine own ease (23)
> In, boy; go first (26)

There is great tenderness here. This is Lear the intercessor, whose purpose is to pray and voice pity for all who suffer, who are vulnerable, who are dispossessed. His debasement has introduced him to the fellowship of the wretched. The momentous speech beginning 'Poor naked wretches' (28-36) represents a milestone on Lear's road to insight. Note the diction of penury, characterising a dimension of need perceived for the first time. 'naked', 'houseless', 'unfed', 'loop'd and window'd raggedness'. He confronts openly his past insensitivity,

O! I have ta'en
Too little care of this! (32-3)

and proposes a redistribution of wealth from the privileged few to the suffering masses.

The sublime beauty of this fellow-feeling is shattered by the reappearance of a terrified Fool and the babble of Poor Tom. Remember that Edgar has forewarned the audience of his disguise; thus they are less likely to cackle at him, and more inclined to enjoy observing his effect on the other characters.

His effect on Lear is crucial. As Poor Tom, Edgar is catalyst rather than character. He is the embodiment of the 'naked wretches' with whom Lear has identified, and in his posture of madness he holds up a mirror to Lear's accelerating derangement; he gives shape and focus to the preoccupations bearing down upon the old man. One may seek for meaning in Poor Tom's babble, but its chief purpose is to present a chorus against which sounds Lear's echoing obsession: the bedlam beggar could only have been bought so low by his daughters (48-9, 62-3, 65-6). Lear conceives of filial ingratitude as universal, the only source of real suffering:

Nothing could have subdued nature
To such a lowness but his unkind daughters. (69-70)

His thoughts are nailed to this cross, and the sheer scale of his preoccupation justifies the claim that this, finally, is madness.

In his sympathy for Poor Tom, Lear gropes for the recurring imagery of depravity: physical disease in 'Now all the plagues' (65) and animal ferocity in 'Those pelican daughters' (74). We have already been jarred by the image of the mouth lacerating the hand; now we contemplate the young pelicans feeding fat upon the flesh and blood of the old. In fumbling for some crazed theme which may make sense of it all, Lear touches upon an idea that recurs elsewhere in the play: sexuality is innately sinful, and in the fullness of time man is justly punished for the carnal pleasure that produced his children (73-4).

Perhaps the Fool feels ousted by the beggar; there is an uncharacteristic level-headedness about his observation, 'This cold night will turn us all to fools and madmen' (78).

Throughout Poor Tom's catalogue of sin and indulgence (84-100), one imagines Lear eyeing him closely. The fascination grows until Lear reaches another stage in his understanding, finding in the beggar's naked-ness an object lesson in what it is to be human: 'unaccommodated man is no more but such a poor, bare, forked animal as thou art' (106-8). Silk, leather, wool and perfume are mere trappings; this is the essence itself. We have here the climax of the clothes imagery in the play. Fine garments have betokened power, wealth, status, the world which hurt Lear and cast him out. We remember that the pitied wretches were 'naked' and that he pondered on their 'raggedness' (28, 31). In wrenching off his own clothes, Lear seeks to root himself in this newly discovered world of irreducible honesty, to identify with Tom and the 'poor wretches', to strive for some sense of his own basic humanity. We think again of the recurring theme of 'nothing'. As this frail old man stands naked, we see how far he has fallen, but perhaps this is the point from which reconstruction may begin. The lunatic who has driven the old king mad has also granted him further insight.

This moment on stage is distressing, difficult, possibly embarrassing. How right not to sustain it, but to distract us with more prattle from the Fool and the entry of Gloucester. The audience will enjoy the accelerated babble of Tom at this point; they are the only ones in the know as father unwittingly confronts son.

Gloucester's promise of fire and food shines through the darkness like a beacon, although it is a sign of Lear's total absorption in his 'mentor' that he ignores it (155-6). His exalting of Poor Tom as an eminent teacher is not entirely unhinged; remember that he *has* learned from him.

Gloucester is the focus of several layers of irony: unaware that he is talking to the man himself, he speaks affectionately of the banished Kent (164-5) and bemoans the fact that Edgar plotted to kill him while the son himself looks on. Edgar thus hears for the first time of his alleged offence and of its effect upon his father: 'The grief hath craz'd my wits' (171). This raises the possibility of Edgar's rectifying the error. As in the case of Lear, the germ of restoration is present.

The closing sequence presses home the parallels between Lear and Gloucester: Lear is in the presence of the disguised Kent, as Gloucester is in the company of the disguised Edgar. Gloucester himself points out the similarity in their cases:

> Our flesh and blood, my lord, is grown so vile,
> That it doth hate what gets it. (145-6)

Gloucester talks of being maddened by his anguish. Ironically, whereas Gloucester ends the scene in emotional agitation (look at the unsettled sentence structure of 163-72), the genuinely mad Lear concludes with measured and elaborate courtesy towards his 'Athenian'.

Act III, Scene v

Summary
Enraged by what he has heard, Cornwall vows revenge on Gloucester, whose earldom he confers on the treacherous Edmund. He then instructs the son to seek out the father so that he may be arrested.

Commentary
A brief pause between 'mad' scenes, implying the passage of time and allowing a necessary respite. Note the change of mood: from the gentleness of Kent and Gloucester to the vindictiveness of Cornwall. We see Edmund at the height of his fortune; having damned his brother, he now undermines and supplants his father. We are sickened by the sanctimonious hypocrisy of Edmund's betrayal, although we recognise another supreme performance:

How malicious is my fortune, that I must repent to be just! (10–11)

Edmund's harping on his finer feelings finds an echo in the 'noble' sentiments pronounced by Cornwall at the end of the scene:

I will lay trust upon thee; and thou shalt find a dearer father in my love. (25–6)

This association cements the links between main and sub-plots. How stange to hear words such as 'love' and 'trust' from so harsh a mouth. Edmund and Cornwall deserve each other.

Act III, Scene vi

Summary
In the outhouse, Lear's fevered mind has continued to toy with vengeance against his daughters, but now he decides that they must be tried. Two stools provide the necessary embodiment. Kent attempts to pacify Lear, but Lear is determined to assemble a bench of justices – himself, Tom and the Fool – and confront his daughters with their evil. Tom and the Fool humour Lear, but Edgar is so overwhelmed that he finds it almost impossible to continue. As Lear eventually sleeps, Gloucester brings news of a plot against his life; he has prepared a cart in which the exhausted King may be carried to Dover. Kent, Gloucester and the Fool bear Lear from the stage. Left alone, Edgar speaks with his own voice.

Commentary
Note the progression by which Lear is led away from exposure: from heath to hovel and now to castle outhouse. There is a sense of rescue under

way, but there are many agonies to live through yet. Kent sets the tone of derangement:

All the power of his wits has given way to his impatience (4-5)

- a mood confirmed by the ravings of Poor Tom (6-8), Lear's desperate assertion that kingship is synonymous with madness (11), and the Fool's acid observation on age superseded by youth:

he's a mad yeoman that sees his son a gentleman before him. (13-14)

There is a demented cacophony about the lines in which Lear envisages vengeance, Poor Tom complains of the 'foul fiend' and the Fool discourses cynically on the folly of trusting (15-19). Yet against this crazed chorus Lear fastens on his decision to try his daughters, as opposed to responding with violence. Is this another stage in his redemption? In the midst of turmoil, does this represent an instinctive fumbling towards order?

The absurdity of the trial is emphasised by the elaborate courtesy with which Lear honours his fellow magistrates: Edgar becomes 'robed man of justice' (36), while the Fool is saluted as 'yoke-fellow of equity' (37). There is no corresponding gentleness towards the 'accused', as Goneril and Regan are denounced as 'she foxes' (23).

The trial is conducted by two madmen and a Fool - a wry comment, possibly, on the reliability of human justice. We must consider the 'danger' of an audience being merely amused by the cavorting on stage, the motley bench of magistrates and the business with the stools. This is off-set by our sense - which the actors *must* make clear - of the Fool and Poor Tom helping Lear to 'work through' his madness; by the solicitous interventions of Kent (34-5, 58-9, 82); by Edgar's distress at Lear's ravings (60-1); and by our satisfaction at hearing Goneril mocked as 'a joint-stool' (52) and the attack on Regan's 'warp'd looks' (53). Observe the veering of Lear's moods: from the calm tone of 47-9, to the hysterical shouts of 54-6, to the pathos of feeling himself shunned even by his pet dogs, to his distressed reflections on the causes of ingratitude:

Then let them anatomise Regan, see what breeds about her heart. Is there any cause in nature that makes these hard hearts? (76-8)

Lear's final preoccupation lies not with punishment but with enquiring into the sources of cruelty. For the moment the rage is spent, as we see the tired submissiveness with which Lear accedes to Kent's tender coaxing:

Make no noise, make no noise; draw the curtains: so, so. We'll go to
supper i'th' morning. (83-4)

His last line is echoed ironically by the Fool, with his final words in the
play:

> And I'll go to bed at noon. (85)

This is an enigmatic utterance, possibly delivered with a broad wink, and
relating perhaps to his early departure from the play, perhaps to pre-
mature death. Is it right for the Fool to disappear at this turning-point?
Would his barbed comments be out of place from now on?

Our relief at Lear's rest – 'Oppressed nature sleeps' (97) – is undermined
by the bustling anxiety of Gloucester. After the turmoil within, we hear
now of threats from without. Lear is again confirmed as victim, denied
rest even at his most vulnerable. Dover is once more a symbol of hope:

> . . . Dover . . . where thou shalt meet
> Both welcome and protection. (91-2)

We must be touched by the departure of Lear. The King who processed
so mightily on to the stage in the first scene, who flounced off in a rage to
seek succour from his other daughter, who rode out in a passion from
castle to heath, who was gently guided to the hovel, led tenderly to the
outhouse, is now carried senseless from the stage by a straggle of faithful
followers.

Edgar's closing address serves the double purpose of emphasising the
anguish of Lear's suffering and the fineness of his own sensitivity. Again
the links between main and sub-plot are highlighted:

> He childed as I father'd! (110)

The hope represented by Dover is strengthened by Edgar's anticipation
of resuming his true identity and seeking reunion with his father. After
the storm, the faintest of lights.

Act III, Scene vii

Summary
Cornwall bids Goneril return to Albany with news of the French landings.
The sisters unite in proposing foul punishment for Gloucester as Cornwall
instructs Edmund to accompany Goneril; what lies in store is not fit for
him to see. Oswald brings news of Lear's escape.

Gloucester is dragged in, tied to a chair and basely abused. Aroused by
their insults, he sees that he has little to gain by further concealment and

admits that he helped Lear to escape so as to spare him more cruelty at the hands of his daughters. With unparalleled viciousness, Cornwall wrenches out one of Gloucester's eyes. As he turns to the other, he is challenged by a servant who cannot abide this violence; he fights with Cornwall, until run through from behind by Regan. Cornwall now turns to complete his vile task and spikes out the remaining eye. Gloucester calls out for Edmund to seek vengeance, only to hear that Edmund was responsible for his betrayal and to realise that Edgar has been wronged. Regan discovers that Cornwall has been wounded in the clash with his servant; she helps her husband from the stage.

Two servants deplore what they have witnessed and determine to follow Gloucester in an attempt to ease his pain and secure for him 'the Bedlam' (Poor Tom) as a guide.

Commentary

A climactic point in the sub-plot, signalled by the grouping of the sinister quartet. Restless activity and gathering pace are shown by the staccato structure of Cornwall's opening lines (1–3). Note also how the daughters' viciousness finds its consummation in:

> REGAN   Hang him instantly.
> GONERIL Pluck out his eyes. (4–5)

This is the measure of them: no softness or feminine warmth here. We may see also a certain irony in that just as the dispute between Cornwall and Albany is set aside for tactical reasons, the seeds of jealousy between the sisters are sown by Cornwall's thrusting together of Edmund and Goneril.

Oswald's account of Lear's escape strengthens the regenerative process, although we are chilled by the rhythmic harshness of:

> Go seek the traitor Gloucester,
> Pinion him like a thief, bring him before us. (23–4)

The crazed trial observed in the previous scene appears the essence of measured justice compared with what now confronts us. The binding of Gloucester to the chair establishes a dreadful foreboding. We must be smitten by the cruel irony of Regan damning Gloucester as 'fox', and even more by the charge that he is 'ingrateful' (28). Consider the dignity of Gloucester's protests. He names them 'your Graces', 'my friends', 'my guests' (30–1). The dues of hospitality are particularly stressed (39–41). Against this grates the fierce bitterness of 'filthy traitor', the humiliating of his venerable age with the disparaging 'corky arms' (29), and the plucking of his beard.

The scene must be visualised: the immobilised Gloucester, the focal point, with the jackals gathered around him. The pace of the lines must be appreciated, with the gathering momentum of questions, jibes, insults and protests in 28–54; this acceleration does much to create the suspense which culminates in Gloucester's confession.

Dover re-echoes throughout 50–4. To us and to Gloucester it is a symbol of hope; to Regan and Cornwall, an enemy foothold. How appropriate is Gloucester's use of the bear-baiting image as he recognises the inevitable: 'I am tied to th'stake, and I must stand the course' (53). How clearly he judges his own vulnerability, and the ferocity of the 'hounds' which surround him. In his confession, Gloucester rises to greatness. We are thrilled by his boldness and his condemnation of Regan and Goneril, observing how reverent gentleness and the sanctity of kingship are set against raking sharpness:

> Because I would not see
> Thy cruel nails pluck out his poor old eyes;
> Nor thy fierce sister in his anointed flesh
> Rash boarish fangs. (55–7)

We shudder at the presentiment of eyes plucked out, and acknowledge again the rightness of the animal imagery. Yet there is reassurance for us in Gloucester's arraigning of them, and in his prediction of revenge (64–5).

Cornwall's image of foot against eye (67), brute force against vulnerability, is more than apt. The blinding of Gloucester is an obscenity, one of the most harrowing and disturbing scenes imaginable. Yet it is right for us to witness it. We have lived through the mental and emotional agony of Lear; now we must endure the parallel physical agony of Gloucester. Possibly, the old man will be slightly turned away, or masked from the audience by his tormentor; yet there will be no missing the physical effort of Cornwall as he lunges at the face, nor the shrieks of agony that follow. Clear, too, is the relish of Regan for her task (70): a bitch on heat, lusting for more blood, more pain. We draw some comfort from the intervention of Cornwall's servant. Regan's stabbing of him represents the final extinction of femininity; her hands, too, are steeped in gore.

'Out, vile jelly' (82) conveys the fullness of corruption; that which is delicate, clear, fragile is debased and ravished. How is Gloucester to deliver 'All dark and comfortless!' (84)? A shriek, a sob, a broken moan? How can we bear the fact that his agony is compounded by the dreadful irony of calling out to Edmund (84–6)? How can we find new depths of loathing for a Regan who delights in revealing the truth about his son (86–9)?

Gloucester's realisation may seem too swift (90–1). This is to quibble, however. Our overwhelming impression must be the dreadful irony that only when he is physically blind does Gloucester achieve insight.

There is no limit to the foulness of Regan. She wants Gloucester thrust out to 'smell his way to Dover' (92) – how appropriate that she should single out the animal sense of smell! We delight in Cornwall's injury, and in the sympathy of the servants, delicately embodied in the restorative purity of the 'flax and whites of eggs' (105) with which they will soothe Gloucester's pain. Thus is the possibility of regeneration maintained. Even after such horrors, not all is bleak; there is still loyalty, still human kindness. The plan to engage the services of 'the Bedlam' contributes to this regrowth, for it will hasten the unification of father and true son.

Act IV, Scene i

Summary
Edgar consoles himself that although his fortunes are low, things can only get better. At this point Gloucester is led on by an old man. He laments his treatment of Edgar, who reflects that here, indeed, are further depths of misfortune. Unaware that he is acquiring the services of his son, Gloucester enlists Poor Tom to guide him to a cliff-top at Dover, implying that this is where he will end his agony.

Commentary
After spiritual and physical torment, a more reflective scene, marked by ponderings on the human condition. Edgar's optimism continues the theme of regeneration, yet complacency is denied by more horror at the sight of his father (9–12).

The old man is to Gloucester as Kent is to Lear: a loyal servant, even at great personal cost. Gloucester's unselfish concern for his safety (15–17) is touching, as is the stoicism and insight of:

> I have no way, and therefore want no eyes;
> I stumbled when I saw. (18–19)

Like Lear, Gloucester is learning from his sufferings, and the paradox here – which is central to the play – has equal relevance to both. When they could 'see', when Lear had his kingdom and Gloucester his eyes, they were 'blind' to the things that mattered, incapable of judging accurately. Insight and true understanding come in the wake of pain and deprivation. Gloucester understands now that comfort and possessions serve us less well than need (19–21). We note the irony of his wish to be reunited with Edgar – standing, unseen, nearby – but, more particularly, the poignancy of the blind man longing to 'see' his son in his touch (23).

As his mind plays on all that he has suffered, Gloucester yields to bleak pessimism, a bitterness which engulfs him:

> As flies to wanton boys, are we to th'Gods;
> They kill us for their sport. (36–7)

There is, he feels, no moral dimension in life, only aimless suffering imposed by indifferent powers. His bitterness is understandable, but he is overlooking his own responsibility: the lechery which spawned Edmund, the short-sightedness which allowed Edgar to be cast out. This is the despair from which his son will seek to redeem him.

Within the imagery of clothing, Gloucester's request for garments for the naked madman may be seen as part of the restoration: a step on the road back. Yet Gloucester is aware of the moral chaos that continues to reign. Note the disease imagery in:

> Tis the times' plague, when madmen lead the blind. (46)

However, this madman 'cures' blindness. As Edgar was a catalyst for Lear, promoting new insights into the human condition, so now he has a similar effect on Gloucester. In becoming the object of Gloucester's generosity, he gives shape to a new concept for which the old man is reaching out - that there is too much inequality and that wealth should be shared:

> So distribution should undo excess,
> And each man have enough. (70-1)

The piercing clarity of this understanding is matched only by Gloucester's distaste for the insensitivity of the rich and gluttonous (67-9). The presence of the mad beggar is instrumental in generating this new perspective, yet we must also consider the impact of the foul behaviour that Gloucester has witnessed among the great and mighty, set against the simple goodness of the old man who led him and the servants who soothed his ravaged face. We should note the parallel between Gloucester's sympathy for the impoverished and the strikingly similar sentiments expressed by Lear in his 'Poor naked wretches' speech (III.iv. 28-36).

This is a difficult scene for Edgar, who is required to play many parts: the moralist, the shocked son, sharing with the audience several asides in which he voices inner doubt and torment (25-6, 27-8, 37-9, 51, 53), the raving bedlamite, the submissive and helpful guide. Yet from this complexity arises greater depth of character than we have witnessed hitherto. The sympathy of 'Bless thy sweet eyes' (53) is a much-needed counterbalance to the obscene 'vile jelly' which scarred the previous scene. The spectacle of Gloucester, secure in the care of his unrecognised son, strengthens the sense of regrowth.

Act IV, Scene ii

Summary
Edmund and Goneril are greeted outside Albany's palace with news of his opposition to them. Goneril dismisses him as a coward and anticipates with Edmund the consummation of their illicit love. She asks him to return to Cornwall to hasten preparations for war, while she assumes power in Albany's place. Edmund leaves with the implication from Goneril that she will be his if he can arrange matters accordingly.

Albany launches a fierce attack on his wife, who scorns him for in-activity while French forces are massing. A messenger brings news of Cornwall's death and of the blinding of Gloucester. Goneril's concern now is that the widowed Regan will be free to compete for Edmund. As she departs to read a letter from Regan, the messenger relates Edmund's treachery. Albany cherishes Glouchester's loyalty to Lear and swears to avenge his eyes.

Commentary

The vileness of Goneril is amply illustrated here, as is the forceful surge of her will. Edmund is virtually silent as she takes the initiative. In just one speech (11-24) she scorns her husband's mildness, reflects on her adultery, determines to wrest authority from Albany, and hints at his murder. There is a venomous appetite here, and we may reflect on the energy of her closing 'instructions' to Edmund. The rank sexuality of 26-8 confirms our loathing. She is befouling another intimate bond; she has no more regard for the marital than for the filial.

The vehemence of the clash between Albany and Goneril is exciting drama, and we delight at Albany's attack; he voices all that we feel about her. The image of the branch detaching itself from the parental tree (34-6) is striking in itself, and part of a pattern of associations by which wholesomeness is associated with the integrity of the natural world.

This is the first scene in which Albany gains real substance as a character; he has expressed reservations before, but now he blossoms in our eyes. He despises the distorted values of the self-seekers:

> Wisdom and goodness to the vile seem vile;
> Filths savour but themselves. (38-9)

Albany's depth of feeling is conveyed by fierce exclamations and incredu-lous questioning. Notice how he continues the animal imagery with 'Tigers, not daughters' (40) and 'monsters of the deep' (49). He sees the unnaturalness well enough. Consider how he juxtaposes 'gracious aged man' and 'reverence' with 'barbarous' and 'degenerate' (41-3). He is our champion now.

The dramatic power stems from the fact that Goneril yields not an inch, indeed returns to the attack herself. The clash accelerates in 59-68, with shorter speeches, open insults ('devil', 'fool', 'fiend'), threats of violence, Goneril's typical mocking of Albany's manhood. Does the arrival of the messenger prevent them from coming to blows? Whatever the case, we surely agree with Albany in:

> Proper deformity shows not in the fiend
> So horrid as in woman. (60-1)

We are conditioned to expect gentleness from women, which renders particularly repellent the corrosiveness of Goneril and Regan.

Cornwall's death, of course, is as much news to us as to Goneril and Albany; this is an effective dramatic device which enables us to share in the response of the players on stage. The pendulum is gathering speed: Lear and Gloucester on their way to Dover, French forces landed, Cornwall dead, Albany asserting the power of goodness, jealousy between the sisters. The significance of the latter point is illustrated well in Goneril's mixed feelings: political satisfaction at Cornwall's death set against sexual jealousy of the liberated Regan. She ends the scene far less confidently than she began it. Both sisters, for different reasons, now lack a husband's support; thus there is an enhanced role for Edmund and greater scope for competing for him.

Albany's satisfaction at Cornwall's death, and his saluting of divine justice, is in part an answer to Gloucester's bleak pessimism of the previous scene:

> This shows you are above,
> You justicers, that these our nether crimes
> So speedily can venge! (78-80)

Vengeance in prospect is precisely the reassuring note on which the scene concludes. Good, we feel, is on the march.

Act IV, Scene iii

Summary
At Dover, Kent meets the gentleman who carried his letters to Cordelia. We hear that France has returned to his country and that Cordelia now leads the invading forces. We also hear of her emotional response to the news of her father's suffering. Kent reveals that Lear is nearby, still deranged though experiencing lucid intervals. Kent will lead the gentleman to Lear, but intends to remain disguised for the moment.

Commentary
Dover at last! Scenes (iii) and (iv) constitute an interlude, a reinforcement of the regenerative process. The chief dramatic purpose of this scene may be to reinstate Cordelia as a character before her reappearance in the next.

The gentleman's explanation of the departure of France is laboured. The real reason for not allowing him to appear is the sensitivity of Shakespeare's audiences to the idea of invasion. He had to stress the 'mission of mercy' aspect, which is accomplished much more easily with Cordelia at the head of the force.

The description of Cordelia's response is beautifully achieved. There was no rage; it is important that she should not be seen as harsh. Nor was her sorrow extravagantly expressed. We remember how she disliked extreme shows of emotion, and appreciate this in the balance of 'patience and sorrow' (17). The lovely metaphor of sunshine and rain (19) – appropriate after the storm – continues this theme of moderation and the healing processes of the natural world. We note her 'ample tear' (13), her 'delicate cheek' (14), her 'ripe lip' (21), and see how an image of subtle bounty is established. To this is added the exquisite beauty of her tears, 'pearls from diamonds dropp'd' (23): her reaction is elevated to an almost sacred reverence in 'The holy water from her heavenly eyes' (31). We have valued the loyalty of the Fool, Kent and Gloucester, and the righteous anger of Albany. Yet how welcome is this sympathy from the wronged daughter who, like Edgar, feels no resentment. To offset the danger of Cordelia's appearing too 'courtly', we have the bewildered expostulations of 26–30 and her reported fleeing in search of privacy (32-3).

It is important for the developing sense of climax that we hear of Lear's arrival at Dover and of his intermittent hold on sanity, his 'better tune' (40). Recovery proceeds, albeit haltingly, seen in the 'burning shame' (47) which makes him refuse to meet Cordelia; there is pathos here, a sense of 'so near and yet so far'.

Kent's damning of the 'dog-hearted daughters' (46) links tellingly with previous animal imagery, and juxtaposes violently with the delicate sensitivity of Cordelia. We are not sure about the nature of the 'dear cause' (52) that will preoccupy him, but we may assume that it is to effect the reconciliation between Lear and Cordelia.

Act IV, Scene iv

Summary
In the French camp, Cordelia is distressed at accounts of Lear's crazed wanderings and sends a party of knights to seek him. The doctor reassures her that he will be able to treat him. Hearing that the British forces are on the march, Cordelia emphasises that her only motive is to seek redress for the wrongs done to Lear.

Commentary
The scene is full of drums, colours and soldiers, yet the tone is of love and sympathy. The warmth of Cordelia's response is all that we have been led to believe, and the presence of the doctor speaks of therapy rather than conquest.

Lear's madness is immediately stressed (2); he has still to live through much pain and rage. The opening imagery – the flowers, the 'sustaining corn', the 'high-grown field' (1–7) – resumes the theme of natural goodness, which is reinforced by the doctor's herbal treatment (13–15) and Cordelia's plea:

> All you unpublish'd virtues of the earth,
> Spring with my tears! (16–17)

We bless the promise of healing sleep – 'Our foster-nurse of nature is repose' (12) – and recall how Lear was denied rest at the end of the frenzied trial scene. The doctor's claim that his herbs will 'close the eye of anguish' (15) calls to mind both Lear's spiritual torment and the physical agony of Gloucester. The 'century' sent in search of Lear (6) parallels reassuringly his cherished retinue.

Cordelia is selflessness personified. We see her scale of values in 'He that helps him take all my outward worth' (10). This is consistent with her character, yet Shakespeare must re-emphasise the point in order to present her as saviour of her father rather than invader of England:

> No blown ambition doth our arms incite,
> But love, dear love, and our ag'd father's right. (27-8)

Act IV, Scene v

Summary

The scene is Gloucester's castle. Oswald arrives with Goneril's message for Edmund, who is not on hand to receive it. He informs Regan that Albany's forces are finally under way. Regan regrets having allowed Gloucester to live, for his scarred face is stirring up feeling against them. Edmund has ridden forth to assess the enemy and to kill his father. Regan, consumed by jealousy of Goneril's letter, attempts to delay Oswald. She tries to persuade him to allow her to open the letter, but he resists. She assures him that she is aware of her sister's amorous intentions and that she herself, as a widow, would be a more suitable choice for Edmund. In a competing gesture she gives Oswald a token to be passed to Edmund, and offers rich rewards if by chance on his journey he should be able to despatch Gloucester.

Commentary

Regan's tactical sense is unbalanced by her lust. After the briefest of questions concerning preparations for battle, her obsessive concern is with Goneril's letter. Native viciousness reasserts itself in her regret that Gloucester was not killed, but most of this scene is taken up with her manoeuvring for Edmund. The awkwardness, the tentative probing, the embarassed defensiveness of Oswald are all embodied in short speeches and stunted dialogue. Examine the broken structure of 19-22, in which Regan hesitates, then reveals her purpose.

We have little time for Oswald, but at least he stands firm on the side of his mistress. Yet, to prevent our viewing him with favour, see how ready he is to fall in with Regan's wish to have Gloucester murdered.

The clinching proof of Regan's neurotic anxiety is that she divulges intimate matters to a servant (30-2). The sisters, so long depicted as animals, are poised to turn their fangs on each other.

Act IV, Scene vi

Summary

Edgar deludes Gloucester into believing that they are climbing to the edge of Dover cliffs. Gloucester kneels and declaims that it is better to end his anguish now. He 'plunges into the void', falling only a short way to the ground where he is kneeling. Edgar now impersonates a bystander on the beach, astonished that anybody should survive such a 'prodigious fall'. Gloucester laments that he is denied even the comfort of death, but Edgar persuades him that he has been saved by benevolent powers. Gloucester is convinced and determines to bear his afflictions in future.

At this point Lear enters, decked with wild flowers. His deranged babbling is incoherent, but there are moments of clarity. As Gloucester weeps at the ranting of his master, Lear finally recognises him. Cordelia's search party finds Lear, who leaves them in his wake as he runs from the stage.

Edgar hears that battle is imminent. As he leads Gloucester in search of refuge, they are discovered by Oswald, eager to kill the old man in accordance with Regan's instructions. Edgar fatally wounds Oswald, who with his last breath beseeches him to pass Goneril's letter to Edmund. Edgar reads the letter and discovers Goneril's plan that Edmund should murder her husband. He hides the letter, intending to show it later to Albany. To the sound of a distant drum, he leads Gloucester to safety.

Commentary

The preceding sequence of short scenes (iii, iv, v) has conveyed a gathering pace. Now this slows as the lengthier scenes (vi) and (vii) show first for Gloucester and then for Lear the regeneration for which we have been prepared.

Edgar's benign duping of his father shows him acting on Gloucester as he did on Lear; to both he brings new understandings. The powerfully visual language (11-24) gives an impression of towering height. Edgar must make his account graphic enough to convince Gloucester, while indicating to the audience that he is pretending; otherwise they, too, may be taken in. If this is achieved, they will enjoy participating with Edgar in the ruse. See how careful he is to keep them on his side by explaining his motive:

> Why I do trifle thus with his despair
> Is done to cure it. (33-4)

Gloucester's obeisance to the 'mighty Gods' (34) and their 'great opposeless wills' (38) projects again the view of man as a plaything of irresistible powers. The audience will enjoy the irony of his blessing to the beloved Edgar. How will they respond to his plunge? With a guffaw or a sympathetic hush? The latter, surely, if what has gone before has been well achieved.

There is another fine performance from Edgar as witness of the plunge. One imagines him kneeling over Gloucester, feeling gently, touching in wonder. The language is as visually striking as before, and breathless astonishment is conveyed by its staccato structure (49–52). Gloucester's despair (60–4) is dispelled by Edgar's insistence on heavenly intervention. 'Thy life's a miracle' (55) is reinforced in 73–4. The audience rejoices with Edgar as the therapy succeeds and Gloucester's restoration reaches another stage:

> Henceforth I'll bear
> Affliction till it do cry out itself
> 'Enough, enough', and die. (75–7)

In his last mad appearance Lear appears to be more insane than ever. Although the flowers continue the theme of healing identification with the natural world, his appearance is enough to shock even Edgar, who shared the agony on the heath: 'O thou side-piercing sight!' (85). The two tortured fathers are now together, in company with the unknown companion who has served them both. Observe how little Edgar and Gloucester say while Lear is on stage: the blind man, with an ear cocked to identify the lunatic, the young man stunned into amazement, are both carried along by Lear's half-crazed, half-perceptive wanderings. Edgar accurately defines them as 'matter and impertinency mix'd: reason in madness' (173–4).

The 'madness' is evident. The 'reason' is manifest in startling flashes of awareness; the journey to self-knowledge continues. Lear understands how he was manipulated – 'They flattered me like a dog' (96–7) – and can judge the storm as a turning point which brought understanding (100–3). He learned not only the deceitfulness of flatterers, but the limits of his own power: 'They told me I was everything; 'tis a lie – I am not ague-proof' (104–5). As Lear shifts to the rhythmic emphasis of verse (107), there is an insistent message: evil, particularly sexual debauchery, is everywhere. What is the point in virtue, when his own self-restraint brought only anguish:

> Let copulation thrive; for Gloucester's bastard son
> Was kinder to his father than my daughters
> Got 'tween the lawful sheets. (114–16)

His estimation of the 'bastard son' is false, but we see the persistence of his pained obsession with his daughters, which accounts for the next compelling theme, the hypocrisy and hidden lustfulness of women:

> Behold yond simp'ring dame,
> Whose face between her forks presages snow . . .

> The fitchew nor the soiled horse goes to't
> With a more riotous appetite. (118-23)

How precisely this captures Goneril and Regan, as they pant over Edmund!

When Lear's harangue breaks down (128-31), Gloucester approaches. Consider the pathos of the two wronged fathers together: Gloucester, anxious to acknowledge his monarch, and Lear, aloof in his madness, referring harshly to Gloucester's blindness (136-50). When Gloucester seeks to kiss his hand, Lear's reply – 'Let me wipe it first; it smells of mortality' (133) – defines how far his sense of kingship has fallen. The expressions of distress from Gloucester and Edgar (134-5 and 140-1) are important, for they direct our own response and limit the possibility of amusement at Lear's cavortings.

Lear's ultimate insight into evil begins with whispers in Gloucester's ear and the childish game of 'handy-dandy'. It then develops into an apocalyptic speech (157-66) which embodies many of his preoccupations: hypocrisy, disgust with sex, abuse of authority, contempt for the wealthy and sympathy for the underdog:

> Through tatter'd clothes small vices do appear;
> Robes and furr'd gowns hide all. Plate sin with gold,
> And the strong lance of justice hurtless breaks;
> Arm it in rags, a pigmy's straw does pierce it. (163-6)

This is a synthesis of many of Lear's obsessions. Its balanced expression is a sign that he is on his way back from madness, a view confirmed by his sudden recognition of Gloucester (176) and his commending of the virtues of patience. We will not miss the pathos of the madman preaching to the blind (177-9), yet the rage is still in him, as he lurches into thoughts of vengeance (185-6).

The discovery of Lear by Cordelia's attendants represents a further progression. There is still delusion in his belief that they have come to imprison him, yet he acknowledges his need for help:

> Let me have surgeons:
> I am cut to th' brains. (191-2)

Recovery is emphasised by the gentleman's soothing reassurance (192, 199, 203-5).

The lengthy scene may be considered in three sections. The first concerns Gloucester's 'fall' and the second Lear's manic commentary on life; the third brings quickening anticipation, with news of the battle and the arrival of Oswald. It is a relief to sense this more vigorous mood, although we should not overlook Gloucester's touching commitment to shun despair (215-17). Such is the success of Edgar's 'treatment', perhaps reinforced by Gloucester's encounter with Lear.

The groundlings would delight in Edgar's role as the muscular swain giving short shrift to Oswald, whose fate throughout the play has involved being tripped, battered and finally killed. His death and the revelation of the incriminating letter constitute further setbacks for the evil ones, to set alongside our growing optimism that suffering will be eased and virtue rewarded.

Act IV, Scene vii

Summary

Cordelia salutes Kent's loyalty to Lear, who, clothed in fresh garments, is carried gently on to the stage. To the sound of music, Cordelia seeks to waken her father with a kiss. She greets him with the fullness of his majesty and as he comes to his senses, kneels in search of his blessing. Lear fumbles towards recognition of Cordelia, humbly acknowledging his age, his weakness, his guilt. Convinced that she must hate him, he is prepared to die at her hands. She has good cause to do him harm; her sisters had none. Cordelia tenderly reassures him and as the doctor counsels rest, leads him gently from the stage. The scene closes with battle imminent.

Commentary

This interlude, Lear's birth into a new life, is the most serene in the play.

The propitious mood is established by the mutual esteem of Cordelia and Kent. The presence of the doctor again conveys healing and solace, a theme strengthened by the news that Lear is asleep and by Cordelia's prayer to the 'kind Gods' (14). Lear's restoration is symbolised by his 'fresh garments'; he has passed from the robes of a king, to the muddy nakedness of the heath, to this reclothing, this renewal. Perhaps we should imagine white robes, almost a baptismal gown?

The music is significant, representing peace and harmony, and recalling Cordelia's recent metaphor of the untuned instrument (16-17). As the modulation is from discord to harmony, so is it from cruelty to the sympathy of Cordelia. Her words define the prevalent mood:

> Restoration hang
> Thy medicine on my lips, and let this kiss
> Repair those violent harms. (26-8)

As she recoils in horror from the thought of Lear's suffering, we note Cordelia's stress on her father's venerable dignity: 'thy reverence' (29), 'these white flakes' (30).

As Lear wakes, note the change from 'my dear father' (26) to 'my royal Lord', 'your Majesty' (44), 'Sir' (48). In every way she seeks to reassure him. We feel the poignancy of his delusion that he is a soul racked in hell and Cordelia 'a soul in bliss' (46). How else to make sense of this not-to-be-believed sight? Examine how Lear's fumbling bewilderment is seen in the hesitant and broken structure of 52-7. The blessing which Cordelia seeks,

> O, look upon me, sir,
> And hold your hand in benediction o'er me (57-8),

is to offset the vile curse hurled at her in the first scene of the play. There is supreme pathos as each kneels to the other, and in Lear's humble sense of vulnerability: 'Pray do not mock me' (59), 'Do not laugh at me' (68), 'Do not abuse me' (77). The speech beginning 'I am a very foolish fond old man' (60-70) is a marvel of tentative and submissive hesitancy. Consider how the negatives – 'I am not in my perfect mind', 'I am doubtful', 'I am mainly ignorant' – are resolved by the wistful assurance of:

> as I am a man, I think this lady
> To be my child Cordelia. (69-70)

The language is stripped of royal pomp; Lear speaks of 'man' and 'child'.

The other characters on stage will reveal by their gestures and expressions that they, like us, are moved by this almost sacred reconciliation. The doctor captures the mood of exhausted serenity:

> the great rage,
> You see, is kill'd in him. (78-9)

The gentle solicitousness of 'Desire him to go in' (81) calls inevitably to mind the harsher occasions when he was cast out. Lear's final words as he is led from the stage are timid, regretful, humbly honest:

> You must bear with me.
> Pray you now, forget and forgive: I am old and foolish. (84-5)

How he has changed from the egocentric monarch. His plea for forgiveness has, of course, already been granted. There can be no more nobly generous words in all of literature than Cordelia's 'No cause, no cause' (76). She, too, has changed. There is no sign here of measured weighing of affection, only the amplitude of reassuring love.

It is right, after such emotion, to change the mood; the brisk shift to a rapid exchange concerning Cornwall's death, Edmund's rise and the approaching battle reminds us that the world moves on and that there are pressing matters in hand.

48

Act V, Scene i

Summary

In the British camp, Regan questions Edmund about his relations with Goneril. When Albany arrives, he reveals his mixed feelings; he has sympathy with Lear, but fears that he must fight to repel the invaders. Regan is determined to ensure that Goneril and Edmund are not left alone. Edgar enters in disguise and passes to Albany the letter from Goneril to Edmund. He begs him to read it before battle and, if victorious, to sound a trumpet, whereupon a champion will appear to assert the truth. Edmund urges haste and Albany departs with the letter unread. Left alone, Edmund cynically reflects on the rivalry of Goneril and Regan. He is determined that there will be no mercy for Lear and Cordelia if they are captured.

Commentary

Edmund is very much in command, yet this scene accentuates divisiveness: between himself and Albany, and between Goneril and Regan. Note the inappropriateness of Regan's badgering questions; they face battle, yet she is dominated by feverish jealousy of Goneril. See how she repeatedly probes (6-9, 10-11, 12-13), how she pries into 'the forfended place' (11), how her loathing rises almost to hysteria:

> I shall never endure her: dear my Lord,
> Be not familiar with her. (15-16)

Goneril reveals corresponding hatred and obsessiveness:

> I had rather lose the battle than that sister
> Should loosen him and me. (18-19)

Their strident competitiveness, exemplified in the manoeuvring over whether Goneril will go to the tent, contrasts starkly with the recreative love shared so recently by Lear and Cordelia.

The 'domestic and particular broils' (30) refer to the clash between Albany and Edmund, and their characters are clearly juxtaposed. Albany is honest, sensitive, torn by the need to fight an invader, while sympathising with him; Edmund is brisk and dismissively sarcastic (28). When Edgar passes the letter to Albany, the sense of climax in prospect is heightened: Albany will be disabused and Edgar prepared to take up arms.

As Edmund turns to the audience with another of his flagrant addresses, his indifference to Goneril and Regan is made clear. To him they are simply 'these sisters' (55), pawns in his power game. In an accurate evaluation hinging on the image of the adder, he captures all of their slyness and capacity for inflicting pain (56-7). 'Which of them shall I take?' (57) embodies his mechanical view; it is merely a matter of weighing

tactical merits and demerits. We note his machiavellian view of Albany
- useful for the battle, but thereafter:

> Let her who would be rid of him devise
> His speedy taking off. (64-5)

Set alongside the seething lust of Goneril and Regan is this cool and
rational calculating.

Thus far the regenerative process has been unhindered; Gloucester has
found new heart, Lear and Cordelia are united, and the evil-doers are at
each other's throats. Now comes a sinister shadow to cast all into doubt:

> As for the mercy
> Which he intends to Lear and Cordelia,
> The battle done, and they within our power,
> Shall never see his pardon. (65-8)

Our confident optimism is built on shifting sands.

Act V, Scene ii

Summary
Edgar promises to return for Gloucester at the conclusion of hostilities.
A short time later, he brings news that the invading forces have been
defeated, and Lear and Cordelia captured. Gloucester sinks once more into
depression, but Edgar again wins him away from 'ill thoughts' and they
depart together.

Commentary
The representation of the battle is perfunctory for several reasons:
(a) Lear and Cordelia are not soldiers; it is the outcome that is important.
(b) The play is already packed with incident; a lengthy battle scene would
 be superfluous.
(c) There remains the problem of identification: sympathising with Lear
 and Cordelia, yet abhorring a French invasion. A brief battle scene
 helps to gloss over this.
(d) It is challenging even now to give on stage a realistic impression of
 warfare; a short battle scene limits the danger of artificiality. Sensitive
 direction will project haste, bustle, panic.
Our chief impression is the lengthening of the shadow cast over Lear and
Cordelia by Edmund's words. The serenity of their reconciliation is destroyed; regeneration has faltered.

Examine the broken structure of Edgar's urgent announcement (5-7).
Set against this the measured despondency of Gloucester, 'No further, sir;
a man may rot even here' (8), which embodies a mood of deepening

pessimism. The antidote must be provided once more by Edgar, in some of the most memorable lines of the play:

> Men must endure
> Their going hence, even as their coming hither:
> Ripeness is all. (9-11)

'Ripeness' replaces 'rot' and stoicism ousts black despair. Edgar's lesson, which Gloucester humbly accepts, is that we must be patient. There is for all things an appointed time which must not be hurried or anticipated.

In a play so much concerned with age and the natural world, the dignified beauty of 'Ripeness is all' lingers in the mind.

Act V, Scene iii

Summary
Edmund enters with Lear and Cordelia his prisoners. Cordelia seeks to console her father but he longs for prison, where they will be able to delight in each other's company. Hurling defiance, Lear is led off with his cherished daughter. Edmund charges an officer to follow and carry out immediately a task for which he will be well rewarded.

On his arrival, Albany requests that Lear and Cordelia be delivered into his safekeeping, but Edmund plausibly explains why he prefers to postpone this. Irritated, Albany emphasises that he regards Edmund as his inferior. Regan disputes this, and Goneril resents the warmth of her praise. As they haggle, Regan declares herself unwell, although she still claims Edmund as her lord. When Goneril demurs, Albany arrests her and Edmund on a charge of treason. Albany calls for a trumpet to be sounded; if no champion appears, he himself will fight Edmund. Regan's sickness grows and Goneril's aside reveals that she has poisoned her. Edgar appears in armour, refusing to give his name but asserting his right to challenge Edmund. They fight and Edmund falls. Albany threatens Goneril with the incriminating letter, but she attempts to brazen out the situation and quits the stage.

The dying Edmund admits his crimes. Edgar identifies himself and recounts his service to Gloucester, to whom he has revealed his identity. He describes the death of his father, overwhelmed by the joyful shock of reconciliation. A servant announces that Goneril has killed herself after confessing to the poisoning of Regan. Kent's arrival recalls Lear and Cordelia, who have been temporarily forgotten. Edmund reveals that he has ordered their execution and a servant is despatched to save them as he is carried off.

Lear enters with the dead Cordelia in his arms. When Kent comforts him, he rounds fiercely on them all, before turning again to his lifeless daughter and revealing that he killed the officer who hanged her. Albany is informed of Edmund's death and announces that Lear will once more be king. Lear, however, is suffering his final agony. He confronts the stark truth that she will 'come no more', then – perhaps fancying that he sees her lips move – he dies.

Pronouncing general mourning, Albany calls on Edgar and Kent to join him in ruling Britain; Kent, however, seeks only to follow his master to the grave.

Commentary

The captivity of Lear and Cordelia, admits the trappings of military power, calls poignantly to mind the white garments and soothing music of not so long ago. Now it has all been soured.

The formality of Cordelia's lines (3-6) reveals a woman struggling for control. They contrast with the joyous affirmation of Lear; confident of her love now, *he* is the bringer of reasuurance. Lear reveals the fullness of his redemption, for at last he has grasped the important things in life – to love openly, to accept love in return, to rejoice in simple pleasures:

> We two alone will sing like birds i'th'cage.
> When thou dost ask me blessing, I'll kneel down,
> And ask of thee forgiveness. So we'll live,
> And pray, and sing, and tell old tales. (9-12)

They will smile at the world of 'gilded butterflies', of 'court news' (13-14) – the world of pomp and status which once meant so much. Now Lear sees its shallow superficiality.

The harshness of Edmund's 'Take them away' (19) moves Lear to passionate defiance. Perhaps we should visualise Cordelia weeping silently against him as his challenge rings out (22-5). Our sharing in Lear's joy is undermined by Edmund's sinister instructions; we understand well and see how precisely he defines his own ruthlessness (31-3). Note the juxtaposition between Albany's fair-mindedness and Edmund's base hypocrisy in justifying the delay by which he hopes to ensure the murder (59-60). By the time Lear and Cordelia are thought of again, it will be too late.

The sniping between the sisters would be absurd were it not for their venom and the sudden illness of Regan, whose bid for Edmund verges on the desperate. Recrimination accelerates to the point where Albany rounds on Edmund as 'Half-blooded fellow' (81) and Goneril as 'gilded serpent' (85); we are reminded here of Lear's image of plating sin with gold, and of the sly treachery which tarnished the happiness of Eden.

For a time, the action proceeds on two parallel lines: Albany's accusation of Edmund alongside the sickness of Regan. As she is led away, the herald initiates a ritualistic spectacle. Imagine the characters withdrawing to the periphery as the proclamation is read, all eyes swivelling to the entry of the masked warrior, the gathering suspense as the challenge is delivered and the response made. For Edgar this is the final disguise;

for the audience it is a microcosm of the battle between good and evil that has dominated the play. They will naturally delight in the condemnation of Edmund – particularly in 'toad-spotted traitor' (137) – and greet Edgar's victory as a restoration of virtue triumphant.

Few will miss the irony of Goneril's complaint of treachery (150), and all will rejoice at the fury of Albany's attack:

> Shut your mouth, dame,
> Or with this paper shall I stop it. (153–4)

Her guilt is demonstrated by her attempt to seize the letter, and her immorality by the claim that she is beyond the reach of justice (157–8). We note, however, the evasive lameness of her departing line (159). She is a spent force.

Is our view of Edmund softened by his frank confession and forgiveness of his opponent (161–5)? Perhaps marginally, but our attention is more on Edgar's self-revelation and dramatic assertion:

> The Gods are just, and of our pleasant vices
> Make instruments to plague us;
> The dark and vicious place where thee he got
> Cost him his eyes. (169–72)

Once again it falls to Edgar to claim that there *is* justice, there *are* benevolent powers. Realistic as ever, Edmund recognises the inevitable. One senses the rhythmic turning of the wheel in:

> Th'hast spoken right, 'tis true.
> The wheel is come full circle; I am here. (172–3)

The embrace of Edgar and Albany symbolises the mutual sympathy of two good men. However, it may be felt that Edgar's lengthy account of his experiences is rather forced. It is helpful for us to hear that he saw his role as 'nursing' (180) his father and his judgement that he 'sav'd him from despair' (190). It is *vital* for us to know that he now regrets having hidden his identity for so long (191), and that Gloucester has died, caught between joy and grief. Nor can we deny the significance of Edmund's response: 'This speech of yours hath mov'd me' (198). Yet one suspects that Edgar's narrative is too protracted. And how ironic that it is during this sequence that time, for Cordelia, is running out.

The pace gathers anew with the arrival of the servant bearing the knife. On hearing that Goneril has poisoned Regan and turned the knife on herself, Edmund observes, with typically sardonic insight, the symmetry of death:

> I was contracted to them both: all three
> Now marry in an instant. (227–8)

It is important to note the legalistic tone of Albany's 'Produce the bodies' (229) and his rejection of pity (230-31), a coldness of tone which will be found again in: 'Even so. Cover their faces' (241). There must be no softening towards two dead vipers.

It is not particularly implausible that Albany has forgotten Lear and Cordelia (235). He has been preoccupied and has no reason to consider them in immediate danger. Examine the significance of 'Yet Edmund was belov'd' (238). A characteristically wry observation, or an indication that he had always felt starved of affection? Whatever the case, we acknowledge Edmund's awareness of his own evil:

> some good I mean to do
> Despite of mine own nature. (242-3)

Edmund's revelation of the danger to Lear and Cordelia throws the stage into a panic. The delayed announcement is a plot device – and should be accepted as such – which delivers a devastating blow just as happiness seems secure. Once again, the cup of comfort is dashed from the lips. There is bitter irony in Albany's 'The gods defend her!' (255).

Lear's entry recalls the processional arrival of Act I. Then he projected pomp and magnificence; now his tormented wail of grief stuns actors and audience alike. Well acted, this scene is almost unbearable. So near and now, for ever, so far. The bird with whom he hoped to sing in his cage lies broken in his arms. The murder of Cordelia is the hideous climax of the cruelty that runs through the play. Regeneration is blasted; all is bleak and sterile. Kent will find the words for it: 'All's cheerless, dark and deadly' (290).

Imagine Lear gently setting down the beloved Cordelia and then remaining crouched over her, turning aside only occasionally to address distracted remarks or replies to the horrified onlookers. Until his death, they, like us, are on the outside looking in at this focus of grief.

As always when an emotion is overwhelming, it becomes the prism through which everything is viewed, and it is impossible to believe that it is not shared by others:

> O, you are men of stones!
> Had I your tongues and eyes, I'd use them so
> That heaven's vault should crack! (257-9)

We will be cast down by the terrible bleakness of:

> She's gone for ever.
> I know when one is dead, and when one lives;
> She's dead as earth. (259-61)

The lurch back to hope with the looking-glass and the feather – because we *know* that it is all over – pains us, as does the rebuffing of Kent:

> A plague upon you, murderers, traitors all!
> I might have sav'd her; now she's gone for ever! (269-70)

The concluding words here, with their blank finality, are an echo of line 259. This, for a moment, is the old, ferocious Lear, which adds to the pathos as he modulates into the whispered coaxing of:

> Cordelia, Cordelia, stay a little. Ha?
> What is't thou say'st? (271-2)

Lear's mind wanders as he reminisces, the proud father, about the softness of her voice, and then exults in the strength which killed Cordelia's executioner (275-7). And then the lapse back into an old man's exhaustion with 'I am old now' (277) and 'Mine eyes are not o'th'best' (279). Given the imagery of the play, this last half-apology is touching indeed.

Distractions continue with tentative recognition of Kent and news of the deaths of Goneril and Regan (278-92). This 'side-tracking' is masterly! Concentration on the body of Cordelia would be both impossible to sustain and unrealistic; the mind *does* shy away from the unbearable. Yet the distractions must not be complete either, and so we see vague deflecting of the proffered information: 'I'll see that straight' (287) and 'Ay, so I think' (292). Lear's grasp on life is weakening as he hovers between the anguish that pierces him and the concern of those who surround him.

For dramatic completeness we need to know of Edmund's death, yet equally we agree with Albany's dismissive response: 'That's but a trifle here' (295). Albany himself rises to a lofty height as he dispenses justice and reasserts the claims of morality (302-4).

Throughout these solemn pronouncements Lear is stooped yearningly over Cordelia, no doubt whispering, touching, caressing. Perhaps it is Albany's promises that prompt Lear's final agonised utterance, for no future benefits can have any meaning when 'my poor fool is hang'd!' (305). The 'fool', of course, is Cordelia - possibly a term of affection from the past - though also calling to mind the only other character for whom Lear has shown affection. In Lear's closing lines (305-11) we witness the cracking of his heart and mind. Observe the number of repeated words and phrases, as he wanders in the bewilderment of pain; the fragmented structure conveys a man panting out his life's breath. There is immense pathos as he fumbles with the absurdity that she of supreme importance lies dead, while puny creatures live on:

> Why should a dog, a horse, a rat, have life,
> And thou no breath at all? (306-7)

Lear's choking sobs sound in the echoing 'never', before the marvellously humble plea for help with his button: a profoundly 'humanising' touch which makes him everyman rather than king. How should we interpret his dying words: 'Look on her! Look – her lips!' (310)? Black despair? Or a belief, at the last, that she is breathing again? The parallel with Gloucester is more satisfyingly complete if we believe that Lear, too, snatches joy at the last.

Edgar's hope that Lear may yet live (312) is stilled by Kent with the pained wisdom of an old man. Enough is enough, they should let him go:

> Vex not his ghost. O, let him pass. He hates him
> That would upon the rack of this tough world
> Stretch him out longer. (313–15)

A sombre stoicism which we see again in Kent's anticipation of his own death (321–2).

The closing lines provide a characteristic ending. The agony is over, evil has been purged, there is hope for the future. The anticipated rule of Albany and Edgar bodes well for a realm which has been convulsed. After his moralising throughout the play, it is appropriate that Edgar's rhyming couplets should conclude it. At the end of a tragedy in which patriarchal age has been so abused, there is reassurance in his reverence for the old and in the self-effacement which is counselled to the young:

> The oldest hath borne most; we that are young
> Shall never see so much, nor live so long. (325–6)

3 THEMES AND ISSUES

3.1 PARENTS AND CHILDREN

Although suffering in *King Lear* escalates to an almost cosmic level, the story finds its roots in a very ordinary situation: the tension between parents and grown children.

At its simplest, the play concerns itself with the expectations of aged parents and the differing responses of their adult children. Macbeth had no doubt about 'that which should accompany old age', which he defined as 'honour, love, obedience'. Lear would certainly say amen to that, although he would add gratitude. His anger with Cordelia stems not just from embarrassment and hurt pride, but also from rage at her apparent ingratitude. As he is progressively broken by Goneril and Regan, his torment resounds on this theme (I.iv.261-3, II.iv.177, III.ii.8-9). Until he begins to learn through suffering, Lear's thoughts are all for himself, of what his children's obligations are to him, of what he has done for them and how it should be rewarded.

The key issue is that both parents and children are confronting a time of transition, of exchange of power and authority. The parents are in decline, the young at the peak of their power and energy. We see two responses from the children. One, from Cordelia and Edgar, is to love and succour their parents, accept their faults, bear no grudge, bide their time. The other, from Goneril, Regan and Edmund, is harsh, egocentric, impatient and domineering. The old are past it, no more than a hindrance and an obstruction. They must be pushed aside and inheritance seized. The best expression of this comes from Edmund, in the words he attributes to Edgar: 'I have heard him oft maintain it to be fit that, sons at perfect age, and fathers declined, the father should be as ward to the son, and the son manage his revenue' (I.ii.73-6). Lear, of course, receives similarly short shrift. In I.iv Goneril speaks repeatedly of his 'dotage'; the point is driven home later by Regan (II.iv.144-8). As his daughters strip him of his retinue, Lear brokenly points out 'I gave you all'. The retort expresses well the philosophy of usurping: 'And in good time you gave it' (II.iv.248). As so often, the Fool drives home the point:

> The hedge-sparrow fed the cuckoo so long
> That it's had it head bit off by it young. (I.iv.217–18)

Lear, Gloucester and Kent cherish a traditionalist view in which family bonds, allegiance, respect and reverence for hierarchy are paramount. Gloucester, surveying the crumbling of Lear's world and his own, laments: 'We have seen the best of our time' (I.ii.116). Edmund, Goneril and Regan are the hard-headed, clear-sighted progressives – the modernists who have no time for antiquated ideas. They are of today and the future, ordering *their* lives and very much in charge of *their* fate.

The opposing attitudes of the children reach their apotheoses dramatically. Goneril and Regan combine to break their father; Edmund contributes to the blinding of Gloucester. *Nothing* will be allowed to stand in their way. A corresponding apotheosis restores the old values; when Edgar leads his blinded father to some retrieval of hope and happiness, when Cordelia reassures the bewildered Lear, they are not being obedient, not responding to any hierarchical imperative. They are simply expressing a love, loyalty and regard too strong to have been undermined by the rash misjudgements of their fathers.

This 'simple tale' of two impetuous old men, betrayed by selfish offspring and redeemed by the love of a wronged child, has a universal relevance. As children we must all come to terms with our attitudes to our parents, to their and our changing needs. As parents we must confront the fact that our children will outgrow us, will supersede.

There is no easy answer, no slick moral. Perhaps, however, we learn with Lear and Gloucester, with Cordelia and Edgar, that the old must not expect to receive all, must continue to give, to understand, to *learn* – and that the young must offer love and respect for as long as necessary. Things cannot be hurried. Ripeness is all.

3.2 MAN AND HIS NEEDS

Through suffering Lear learns a new valuation of himself and the human condition. It is a valuation nowhere in evidence in the early stages of the play, which develop in a mood of relentless materialism, of that which can be counted and measured. Gloucester and Kent talk of the division of the kingdom; Lear wants his daughters to express the dimensions of their love; the actual number of knights becomes a crucial symbol of self-hood. A man, it appears, is what he owns, an expression of his chattels. Harried by his daughters into justifying his need for a retinue, Lear's speech beginning 'O reason not the need' (II.iv.262) is magnificently moving, but breaks down in confusion. He seems to be asserting that man needs superfluous items in order to mark him off from animals, but the line of thought will not hold. It is, in any case, a view that he will come to reject.

It is during the storm that Lear stumbles towards a conception of what man really is, what his true needs are. From raging against hypocrites, he turns to sympathy for the impoverished – 'Poor naked wretches' (III.iv.28) – before becoming one himself by dragging off his clothes in emulation of Poor Tom. He sees through the world of surface impressions; he knows and demonstrates that he is one of the lowliest. Lear continues to learn – of the need for honesty, simplicity and openness. It is a theme which culminates in his reunion with Cordelia and particularly in his 'birds in the cage' speech (V.iii.8-19). The important thing is to be with those one loves and trusts, to seek and offer forgiveness as may be required, to delight in each other's company.

And what of man's justice? We find in *King Lear* that the wealthy and mighty do not guarantee even-handed justice; those with the whip-hand of power and authority often abuse it. Consider Lear's 'trial' of his daughters' affection and his gross punishment of Cordelia and Kent; the flaying of Lear and Gloucester by the newly installed high and mighty; the cruel death of Cordelia. Where is the justice in all this? The crazed trial of III.vi somehow projects the falsity of it all, while Lear's outburst in IV.vi against the 'rascal beadle' and 'robes and furred gowns' is a fulminating attack on evil in office. Gloucester contributes to this understanding in that his blinding, by the rich and elevated, is a catalyst which attracts simple goodness from the lowly servants and the old man who guides him. This is why, like Lear, he comes to see the importance of sharing wealth and 'undoing' excess (IV.i.70-1). The best guarantee of justice seems to lie not in setting one man over another, but in mutual sympathy and regard for each other's dignity and needs.

Are we to infer that lusting after riches and possessions is ultimately self-defeating? The sour deaths of Cornwall, Regan, Goneril and Edmund certainly seem to point to this. On the other hand, Lear and Gloucester – two old men who suffer and lose so much – seem in a sense to be victorious, for they achieve some grasp of man's need for candour, justice, truth, patience, forgiveness and love.

3.3 KINGSHIP

> Take but degree away, untune that string,
> And, hark, what discord follows! (*Troilus and Cressida*)

For the Elizabethans, the monarchy was not simply a functional role. It was a crucial part of a hierarchy ordained by God himself which encompassed the divine, spiritual, human, animal and material world. Everything had its allotted place in this sequence. To disrupt was to invite chaos. The king was God's voice on earth, and any attempt to wrest the throne from him would lead to turmoil. This was not some remote theory. That so many of Shakespeare's plays are concerned with the overthrow of kings – and that upheaval invariably follows – is a reflection of the significance of the concept, and of Elizabethan anxiety about the succession to the Queen.

The Elizabethans would have found it difficult to understand Lear's abdication. Even worse was to divide the kingdom and thus create scope for future rivalry; such a deed could not be countenanced by a people for whom the internecine bloodletting of the Wars of the Roses remained a folk memory. Shakespeare's contemporaries would understand Lear's problems: a tired old king with no son to inherit, his preferred daughter unattached. But they would have seen no answer but for the king to endure; God had placed him on the throne and, in the fullness of time, Gold would remove him. If they understood Lear's dilemma, they would understand even better the chaos springing from his wrong-headed decision.

There is a more personal perspective in which we must view this theme of kingship. The play seems to indicate that the elevation of the throne can distort the person who occupies it. Lear has been met for so long with sycophancy that he can no longer distinguish between sincerity and falsehood. He has for so long been obeyed in every particular that he cannot abide the slightest delay in the observance of his wishes. That which in the young king might have been forthright and assertive has now degenerated into the vain, harsh and imperious.

Is this likely to happen to all kings, all rulers, all leaders? Perhaps, but what we know for certain is that Lear has to undergo an agonised peeling away of accumulated layers of insensitivity and obtuseness before finding himself. Would he have needed to do so if he had been a humble servant rather than a sovereign? It seems hardly likely. Is a king a victim as well as a ruler?

3.4 PAGANISM AND PESSIMISM?

We are constantly reminded in *King Lear* that we are in a pre-Christian era. There is no appeal to an overtly Christian ethic, no calling upon God – only upon the gods. And their names are frequently conjured. We think of Lear's invocation of supernatural powers in his outburst against Cordelia (I.i.110–13). Many of the characters turn to the gods in similar fashion. Have they ordained it so? Do they care? Will they help? Apollo and Jupiter are invoked, and Gloucester (I.ii.107–22) is convinced of the influence of the stars on their lives, a view later echoed by Kent (IV.iii. 33–6).

There is a prevalent ethos of pagan deities surveying the world of puny men. To what effect? *Are* they involved? In his agony, Lear would certainly have it so:

> O heavens
> If you do love old men . . .
> Make it your cause. Send down and take my part! (II.iv.187-90)

In his despair, Gloucester sees nothing but indifferent cruelty in the powers above:

> As flies to wanton boys are we to th'gods;
> They kill us for their sport. (IV.i.36-7)

This seems to be countered by Edgar, as he stands over the vanquished Edmund (V.iii.169-70). On hearing of the deaths of Goneril and Regan, Albany speaks assuredly of 'This judgement of the heavens' (V.iii.230), and learning of the danger to Cordelia, calls out: 'The gods defend her!' (V.iii.255). The answer? A distracted Lear carrying the dead body of his daughter. The gods, it seems, are not so just after all. After Lear's death, there is no further mention of supernatural powers; it is for human beings to pick up the pieces.

The fact is that the play offers no solution to the question of how far 'the gods' influence lives on earth. There are no tablets of stone, no heavenly referees to deal out rewards or punishment equitably, no certainty; only confusion about an existence which brings deserved punishment to Cornwall, Edmund, Goneril and Regan – but also sweeps away Cordelia.

The only 'certainty' seems to be that men do not entirely shape their own destiny; Lear, Gloucester and Cordelia in no sense deserve the disproportionate suffering that is their lot. Yet nor is the opposite true; this is not a world of random occurrences. Men may not finally determine what happens to them, but they do contribute to it. Lear's vanity and rashness unleash a havoc that brings madness, war and the death of his beloved daughter. Gloucester's adultery, so flippantly discounted, costs him his eyes. Yet as we are finding some shape in this, we agonise again over the death of Cordelia, which happens by chance, because she was not thought of in time. It seems that although the gods themselves may not kill us for their sport, they do not intervene to prevent us killing each other.

Is the play, then, fundamentally pessimistic? It seems hard to disagree when one reviews the catalogue of evil: fathers are betrayed, families disrupted, marriages defiled, the country plunged into dissension and war, bestial cruelty goes largely unchecked, everyone is a sinner, justice is a sham, flawed but largely good people are doomed along with the evil. Yet this is a play in which perspectives shift too readily to permit confident generalisation; there is often another side to the coin. Consider the theme of Nature. Edmund's egocentric goddess? Certainly. The howling storm which lashes Lear? Beyond doubt. But think then of Nature as the earth mother upon whom Lear calls (I.iv.277), Nature as the sure standard of rightness espoused by Lear and Gloucester, Nature as the soothing balm of Acts IV and V.

There are other counterbalancing elements: throughout the play, the loyalty and moral probity of Kent and Edgar; Albany growing in stature to become a leader of truth and justice; Lear and Gloucester learning important lessons as they writhe; above all, the reliable and unforced love of Cordelia. As she watches over her father, clothed in his fresh garments, waking to the accompaniment of music, we are assured that love will abide, that in cherishing each other lies our best hope of redemption. It is an assurance to which we may cling in spite of the bitterness of her death.

The picture, then, is not one of unrelieved pessimism. The play closes at a peak of suffering, but typically, there is a feeling that the worst is past, the evil is burnt out, better men are now in power and a brighter future beckons. It has been remarked that *King Lear* is a Christian play about a pagan world. This is perhaps a simplification, but we may concede that the 'sympathetic' characters experience several of the basic teachings of Christianity: the primacy of love, the possibility of redemption, the assurance that evil – no matter how corrosive – will not ultimately prevail.

4 TECHNIQUES

4.1 CHARACTERISATION

Lear

> . . . a man more sinned against than sinning (III.ii)

Lear's development from arrogant self-absorption to a humble revaluation of life justifies A. C. Bradley's dictum that the title could well be 'The Redemption of King Lear'. The character sketch which follows charts this evolution scene by scene. Key stages are identified by asterisks.

I.i   The imperious king, hopelessly unrealistic in proposing to divide his kingdom. Vanity and love of flattery are clear in the 'love test'. Naive lack of insight into his daughters. Raging petulance. Selfishness of seeking to retain the trappings of power (133-7). Autocratic obstinacy. Absurd blunder of driving out Kent and Cordelia.

I.iii   More ill-judged rashness – striking of Goneril's servant.

I.iv   Kent's devotion suggests a more positive side. Lear self-pitying, refusing to ponder on the Fool's pining for Cordelia. Affectionate to Fool, but won't tolerate criticism.

        *Clash with Goneril initiates crisis of identity (227-31).

        *He understands that he wronged Cordelia (268-73).

I.v   *More understanding: 'I did her wrong' (25).

        *Fear of madness.

II.iv   Instability before meeting Regan and Cornwall. Still preoccupied with retinue and status.

        *Begins to assess the human condition: 'O reason not the need!' (262).

        *More humble view of self: 'a poor old man' (270).

        *Fear of madness.

III.ii The last of the egocentric Lear, as he calls down destruction on the world.

    *Attack on hypocrisy and hidden evil; begins new assessment of society which will continue until IV.vi.

    *Accepts that he has sinned (60).

    *Sympathy for the Fool.

    *Insight into real need: 'The art of our necessities' (70-1).

III.iv *More moralising on degrees of suffering (6-12). Final outburst against ingratitude (12-20).

    *Repeated fear of madness (21).

    *Sympathy for Fool. Need to pray: 'Poor naked wretches' (28-36). Now looking towards others, rather than self.

    *Real madness: obsessed with Tom's 'daughters'.

    *'Unaccommodated man . . .' (106-9) – he identifies with the human condition at its most basic.

III.vi *Even in deranged trial, struggling for order, enquiring into the nature of cruelty.

IV.iii *Lear's reported shame at his treatment of Cordelia (43-8).

IV.vi *Still mad but understands past flattery, his own vulnerability (105).

    *Sees evil everywhere, particularly in women.

    *Rails against hypocritical evil in the rich and powerful. Appreciates the deceptiveness of appearances.

    *Recognises and preaches to Gloucester.

The end of Lear's madness

IV.vii *The new Lear reborn in the presence of Cordelia. No false pride: 'I am a very foolish fond old man' (60). Kneels to Cordelia. Accepts his sin and her right to punish. Seeks reconciliation (84-5).

V.iii *Lear confident even in defeat because he has found new values by which to live: the joy of unforced love, companionship and mutual trust. Cordelia's death devastates the newly 'redeemed' Lear. Whether or not one accepts that he dies a happy death, he certainly dies a better man. The vain tyrant has been transformed into a simple man who, albeit for the briefest of intervals, judges well, sees clearly, loves truly.

Cordelia

So young, my lord, and true. (I.i)

Cordelia's impact on the plot is profound, both in initiating and concluding the action. She is spoken of as a symbol of virtue, but there is more iron to her personality than this would imply. She has a retiring disposition, and abhors hypocrisy and false shows of affection. Yet she *could* have humoured her father, offered some 'tactical reassurance' to an old man; there is more than a hint of her father's obstinacy. She is important as a catalyst in provoking the frenzied rashness of Lear and highlighting the pretences of Goneril and Regan. She is also a shrewd judge of her sisters' cant (I.i.270–83). During her absence Cordelia is kept alive in our imaginations by:

(a) the reference to the Fool's affection for her (I.iv.73–4);
(b) Lear's growing awareness of having wronged her;
(c) her letter to Kent (II.ii).

She is established in the central section of the play as a symbol of hope.

When Cordelia is reunited with Lear, we see that she too has changed. In an atmosphere conditioned by the healing presence of a doctor and the soothing influence of music and sleep, we see how much she has mellowed. No longer inflexibly assertive, she seeks forgiveness and blessing. There is no resentment; past harshness is met with soothing and renewing love. It is typical of her unselfishness that in defeat she thinks only of Lear (V. iii.3–6), and typical of her role as catalyst that her lifeless form causes his death as surely as once her insistent honesty provoked the rage that began it all.

Goneril and Regan

> . . . dog-hearted daughters (IV.iii)

There is nothing tender about these 'unnatural hags' (II.iv). The animal imagery that characterises them is certainly appropriate as they abuse every decency and lacerate anything which stands in their way.

Yet they are not simply a 'matching pair'; there *is* differentiation between them. Goneril is the more formidably assertive in her vileness, more of a driving force; Regan is a follower, though she is capable of any viciousness once a lead has been given. At the end if I.i it is Goneril who suggests that they collaborate in dealing with Lear, while Regan is inclined to prevaricate (308–9). It is Goneril who orders the provocation of Lear (I.iii), who first confronts him, unflinching in the face of his curses. By contrast, Regan chooses to be away from home when Lear arrives. While Goneril dominates her husband, Regan is very much under the sway of hers. When confronted by Lear (II.iv), Regan is inclined to be placatory, going on the attack only after the arrival of Goneril. Yet note that it is Regan who orders the doors to be bolted against her father, and exults in the blinding of Gloucester.

Their relationship is tenuous, and there can be little surprise when they turn on each other in their lust for Edmund: unnatural daughters panting after an unnatural son. Even here, Goneril is the dominant force. Regan is at least a widow, but Goneril is happy to enter an adulterous relationship, to plot against her husband's life, to poison Regan, to kill herself when all is lost. She sours all that is sacred, violates every relationship.

The evil of Goneril and Regan is an operative force from the beginning of the play; it is not something into which they develop. And it is an evil with no relieving feature: squalid and base, with no trace of ill-starred magnificence. 'Tigers, not daughters', touched with the mark of Cain.

Edgar

> Give me thy arm;
> Poor Tom shall lead thee. (IV.i)

Is Edgar a *real* character or simply a sequence of roles – naive and gullible victim, Poor Tom, moralist, rustic peasant, dutiful son, avenging knight, future leader?

There is no denying the functional importance of Edgar. He is a prime link between the main and sub-plots: together with Kent in the stocks, Edgar in the mud symbolises the downfall of the old world of traditional values: his moralising soliloquies (III.vi and IV.i) clarify the issues, re-assert standards: above all, in his role as the bedlam beggar he *acts upon* the minds and emotions of both Lear and his father, radically altering their perception of the world.

But what of him as a man? He is ingenuous at the beginning, thereafter flexible and versatile, harbouring no resentment, never guilty of a base word or action, and concerned only to help those who suffer: someone who makes the most of difficult circumstances, who genuinely believes in providence, who can identify the causal link between his father's promiscuity and his blinding. Yet there *is* enough to humanise him, to prevent the appearance of a priggish do-gooder. We think of the times when his disguise is threatened by his tears (III.vi.60–1; IV.i.51), of his lusty delight in drubbing Oswald (IV.vi), of his manly determination to challenge Edmund, of his self-criticism at delaying the revelation of his identity to Gloucester, and of his authoritative stance at the end of the play.

There *are* too many roles for Edgar to achieve real depth of character, but he is not a mere cipher. And let us not forget the appropriateness of setting against assertive evil on the one hand a correspondingly assertive goodness on the other.

Edmund

> All with me's meet that I can fashion fit. (I.ii)

There is all the difference in the world between the evil of Goneril and Regan – dour, stark, mean-minded – and the evil of Edmund, which has an almost magnificent vitality and elan. His first appearance in I.ii reveals all. He scorns traditional attitudes, establishing himself as a crusader in the cause of amorality. There is tremendous energy and vigour here: marital fidelity and family ties are swept aside. Self-confident and poised, for Edmund a man is what he makes himself, especially 'by wit' (I.ii. 189). His pride in his cunning is justified; Edgar and Gloucester are slickly manipulated, while Cornwall and Regan are smoothly incorporated into his plans (II.i.15-16). Other people are there to be used; he plays off Goneril and Regan against each other. Yet nobody is allowed to use *him*, as we see when he fights shy of Goneril's suggestion that he should murder Albany (V.ii.62-5).

Such single-mindedness makes him a successful military leader, concerned with results and not the niceties of principle. Yet we must beware of glamourising this dangerous man, and remind ourselves that he does callously abuse those who are closest to him. He delivers Gloucester into the hands of Cornwall and Regan; he later rides out to apply the final murderous thrust to his own father; he calmly orders the execution of Lear and Cordelia. He is attractive in his zest, perhaps, yet lethally unscrupulous.

Does the scale of Edmund's evil make his 'conversion' in the final scene rather feeble? We note his confession and his forgiveness of Edgar (V.iii. 161-5); his compassionate response to the account of Gloucester's travails (198-9); the implication that he had, perhaps, been starved of affection (238-40); his revelation of the death sentence on Lear and Cordelia (242-6); and we remind ourselves that many of the major characters *do* change radically during the course of the play.

Yet one suspects that Edmund's conversion is too sudden, too sweeping to be convincing: that such a vibrantly amoral man would more characteristically have stood hurling defiance from the threshold of eternity.

Gloucester

I stumbled when I saw (IV.i)

As Lear has to go mad before he can understand, so Gloucester has to be blinded before he can 'see'. There is no doubting the opaqueness of his vision beforehand. In his opening conversation with Kent he is a garrulous and morally slipshod old man, dismissing past promiscuity and exhibiting gross insensitivity towards Edmund. His bemoaning of recent events (I.ii.110) reveals that his heart is in the right place, but we must be struck by the naivety and rashness that he shows in misjudging his sons. He is 'A credulous father', whose superstitiousness (I.ii.107-18) is entirely in character.

Gloucester is well intentioned but weak. When Kent is stocked (II.ii) he attempts to press Lear's case, while not wishing to provoke Cornwall. His nervousness regarding 'the fiery quality of the duke' is specified in

II.iv. Gloucester *is* loyal to Lear, but at first tries to keep his options open, deferring to Cornwall and only committing himself fully to Lear when he hears of the French invasion (III.iii.8–20).

He rises in our estimation when he leads Lear to his castle out-house and then secures his escape, and certainly achieves stature in the desperation with which he finally rounds on Regan and Cornwall (III.vii.55–65). His blinding secures for him an elevated place in our regard. He is an essentially unimpressive man, but he has stood out against the forces of darkness and suffered most dreadfully.

In the aftermath of his agony, Gloucester is overwhelmed: he can't cope, he despairs, he seeks suicide. He perceives no link between past sins and present suffering. He considers himself an innocent victim, crushed at random (IV.i.36–7). This moral obtuseness will remain, but he *is* in a limited sense redeemed by Edgar: he is won away from suicide to a saddened and stoical wisdom, an understanding that man must abide. His death, caught between joy and anguish, represents an appropriate ambivalent conclusion to the life of a fundamentally affable though flawed and unassertive man.

Albany

Worthy prince . . . (V.iii)

Our first impression of Albany (I.iv) is that he prefers to conciliate rather than to confront. His 'Pray, sir, be patient' (263) and 'My lord, I am guiltless' (275) project the moderation of a concerned and dignified man. Yet at this early stage – tentative and governed by his 'great love' for Goneril – he defers to the strident self-will of his wife.

When next we see Albany (IV.ii) he has found his voice. His fierce attack on a wife who now repels him is thrilling. His mixed feelings about the battle (V.i) reveal the sensitivity of an honourable man caught in a moral dilemma. In the final scene, Albany is both mighty warrior and dispenser of justice. He has the courage to challenge Edmund and rounds vehemently on Goneril with the sordid letter. We observe his warmly emotional response to Edgar's account of his experiences, and the severity with which he excludes sympathy for the evil dead (230–1, 295). He has the voice of authority as he sets forth his plans for the future: a leader, indeed, who has lived through evil times without being tainted. Goneril once taunted Albany as 'milk-livered' (IV.ii.50), relishing her insult, but ignoring the fact that milk soothes, nourishes and promises future growth. She spoke more truly than she knew.

Cornwall

. . . the fiery duke (II.iv)

Cornwall is a man with no redeeming feature. He first develops as a character when he stocks Kent (II.ii), showing his arrogance and determination not to be outfaced. He grows further in our consciousness as a result of Gloucester's fear of his rages (II.iv.90-3). He condones the harrying of Lear by Goneril and Regan, and appropriately confirms his baseness when he secures the services of Edmund. His bestial cruelty to Gloucester needs no comment, and when his servant rises against him, he expresses our revulsion and loathing for an unfeeling and harshly ruthless man.

Kent

O thou good Kent (IV.vii)

There is no radical development in the character of Kent. He remains throughout the blunt man of action, outspoken and unfailingly courageous. The boldness with which he challenges Lear in the first scene is matched only by the devotion with which he serves him thereafter. On stage at the end as he is at the beginning, Kent is the voice of sound commonsense, the standard of loyalty by which others are judged.

Yet we must not dismiss him as the dogged follower, for there is more to him than this; think, for instance, of the delighted exuberance with which he beats Oswald and then roundly insults Cornwall (II.ii). When he watches with Lear through the dark torment of the heath, we must be touched by the sturdy tenderness of his concern:

> LEAR: Wilt break my heart?
> KENT: I had rather break mine own. (III.iv.4-5)

Cordelia's thanks to Kent in IV.vii express our own regard, and are deflected with typical modesty.

At the end of the play, Kent is a poignant figure. All that he has worked for is to reveal himself to Lear, to be united with his master. And at the moment of consummation, everything is snatched away. We may imagine his voice breaking on 'Is this the promised end?' (263). Suddenly we are aware of his age: a saddened man, crushed by the death of Lear and now sombrely contemplating his own.

The Fool

A bitter Fool . . . (I.iv)

As a character, the Fool is hardly 'fleshed out' in our minds, although there are some points which give him a little depth: his pining for Cordelia (I.iv.73-4); Lear's affection for him (I.iv.106) - perhaps the son he never had; his fundamental loyalty to Lear (II.iv.81-2); and his cowering in the storm, which projects a sense of physical fragility.

Nonetheless, it is as *function* rather than *character* that the Fool is important. His basic role is that of the chorus, commenting on the action and adding point to our perceptions. In this context, for all his facetiousness, he joins Cordelia and Kent as a third voice of commonsense and sanity in the wake of Lear's aberration. In I.iv and v he harps on his master's foolishness in giving everything away and setting his daughters in authority over him. There is verbal wit and prattling enough to add a veneer of humour, but the message is insistent, and sharp enough for a wincing Lear to threaten the whip (I.iv.111). Nor should we deny that there may be some malice and spitefulness in the Fool's taunts, perhaps resentment at the expulsion of Cordelia.

Of course, the Fool may also be appreciated as a jester, with his babbling, cavorting and snatches of song. One can imagine the groundlings in particular enjoying such salty ribaldry as we find at the end of I.v. There is no doubt that his levity often serves to release tension in particularly anguished situations, and in the crazed trial scene of Act III it is dramatically important that the Fool attracts the audience's laughter to himself and away from Lear.

It is paradoxical that the Fool helps to drive Lear mad – and to find his salvation. The insanity which Lear already fears at the end of I.v. stems largely from the harsh treatment of Goneril, but also from the acid probing of the Fool. Yet as the Fool clings to Lear – part comfort and part goad – on the heath, he joins Poor Tom and the storm itself in combining to break down Lear's self-centredness and unawareness of the poor. He is instrumental in helping his master to find a new vision of life and is thus an integral part of the moral process of the play.

Why does he disappear? Because he is no longer needed. Throughout the third act he is overshadowed and gradually supplanted by Poor Tom. When Lear has lived through the climax of his agony and is able to sleep, he is in effect embarking on his recovery, on the painful road to self-awareness and understanding. There is no need now for a wise and caustic Fool to keep re-opening the wound.

4.2 STRUCTURE

The plot offers no backward glance at Lear's earlier life; we are concerned only with his dire misjudgement and the upheaval consequently unleashed. Unusually, the tragic error occurs right at the beginning of the action, thus concentrating all our attention on Lear's subsequent decline and fall.

Although the numbering of act and scene divisions is the work of later editors, Shakespeare was, of course, envisaging his play as a sequence of dramatic episodes, and it is possible to make several general observations about the nature of these. In the first two acts, the plot develops with a degree of pace. The third act, with the agony of Lear and Gloucester, is much slower – a tortured situation, rather than a continuing of momentum. The fourth act, with its variety of scenes and situations, and the fifth, packed with incident, revive the pace as we are carried onward to longed-for reconciliation and ultimate tragedy.

In terms of plot structure, *King Lear* is often described as the most complex of Shakespeare's tragedies. If this is so, then the cause must lie in one of the play's most striking characteristics: the parallelism between main and sub-plots. There is, of course, a danger in talking of main and sub-plots, because it fosters a false sense of two *separate* lines of action, whereas the two strands are closely related and interwoven; indeed, the characters of the sub-plot – Gloucester, Edmund and Edgar – are centrally involved in the main action.

Nonetheless, there *is* a distinction to be drawn between the main and the secondary action which will allow us to consider points of similarity as follows:

(a) Both plots centre on an elderly father and on children who are now adult.
(b) Both fathers are stubborn and strong-willed.
(c) Both lack the judgement to see through selfishness and to value true worth.
(d) Both cast out the children who truly love them and are deluded by the false.
(e) Both suffer tragically as a result of their rash misjudgement.
(f) Both are thrust out into the open countryside.
(g) Both fear madness, though it is only Lear who succumbs.
(h) Both old men are accompanied at different times and ultimately together by the disguised Edgar.
(i) Lear finds in his mental anguish that he wronged Cordelia, as Gloucester finds in his physical agony that he abused Edgar.
(j) Both old men experience a process of renewal.
(k) Lear is succoured by the wronged Cordelia, as Gloucester is supported by the wronged Edgar.
(l) Both old men die of emotional shock.
(m) Both plots exhibit rivalry between the children: the hideous sisters in the main plot and the brothers in the secondary line of action.

The parallels are strong indeed, though with sufficient differences between the plots to prevent the one from becoming a mere reflection of the other. But is it all dramatically justifiable? It is sometimes asserted that the sub-plot crowds the stage with too many characters and over-complicates the situation to the point where even Shakespeare is struggling to orchestrate the action in its entirety. To this, supporters of the sub-plot respond with the claim that it gives scope and resonance to the action and themes of the play; that each plot provides an illuminating perspective on the other and helps to convey a sense of immense scale.

In other words, what happens to Lear is not a single, grotesque aberration, for something very similar happens to Gloucester. We are more disturbed and outraged by each of the stories because we are denied any consoling sense of its uniqueness. The great critic, Schlegel, has expressed this well: 'Were Lear alone to suffer from his daughters, the impression would be limited to the powerful compassion felt by us for his private misfortune. But two such unheard-of examples taking place at the same time have the appearance of a great commotion in the moral world'.

Some brief comment is needed on alleged flaws or improbabilities in the plot, although critics who identify these are often guilty of forgetting that we are dealing with a play, not a meticulously logical construction. Here, then, are some of the most common complaints, with a few words of comment or rebuttal on each:

1. Why should Edgar take to his heels without wishing to plead with or explain to his father? The obvious answer is that he fears for his life!

2. Why should Gloucester wish to be taken to Dover, when suicide would be possible anywhere? Apart from the dramatic necessity of assembling all of the main characters at Dover, one must also consider that would-be suicides often reveal obsessive inclinations concerning the manner of the intended death.

3. Why does Edgar delay for such a long time before revealing his true identity to his father? Edgar himself accepts that he was wrong in this (V.iii.191): in fact, that he had miscalculated. It seems that he is leading Gloucester through a course of 'therapy' to rid him of his despair, and that he wishes this to be complete before he reveals himself. Perhaps also there is an element of Gloucester being made to undergo a term of 'punishment' for his faults.

4. Why do we lose sight so suddenly of the Fool? We are not dealing here with a biographical documentary; it is not at all inconsistent with the role of the Fool that he should disappear when he is no longer needed, when his very *persona* would be gratingly inappropriate.

Other objections are raised, but this selection should give some impression of the kind of reservations expressed – and of how they may be countered. The crucial point is that none of these so-called flaws would occur to us in performance, which is surely the acid test.

Nor are we disconcerted in performance by Shakespeare's intentional vagueness regarding place and time. After the dreadful blunders of the first two acts, we are concerned not so much with the development of a story-line as with the mental and emotional states of Lear and Gloucester; as they suffer their torments, seeking to find some pattern and meaning in life, we move far away from the parameters of conventional dramatic realism. In this context, to adhere to the niceties of geographical place and chronological time sequence would be irrelevant. Indeed, it would prove a distracting factor, as will be seen if we consider too realistically the matter of the French invasion.

We are encouraged – rightly – to view this as a response to the ill-treatment of Lear, but if we consider too closely, we realise that France and Cordelia must have taken the first steps towards invasion *before* hearing of the full magnitude of Lear's suffering; as early as Act II, scene ii we find Kent reading Cordelia's letter and hinting that she is to take action, and this is before Regan rejects Lear, before the agonies on the heath. What are we to think, then? That France invades in order to regain Cordelia's inheritance? Surely not, as this would gravely affect our view of Cordelia's motivation, particularly as she so forcefully discounts any selfish motive in taking up arms. If we are insisting on realism of time sequence, Shakespeare could only cater for this by slowing up the plot development, allowing the fullness of Lear's suffering and *then* sufficient time for the news to reach France.

This, clearly, would draw out the structure of the play intolerably. It is much better to accept the vagueness of place and time for what it is: a dramatic technique which strips away inessentials and focuses our attention on the emotional impact of the play.

4.3 VERSE AND PROSE

He was not of an age, but for all time. (Ben Jonson)

Few would argue with Jonson's tribute, but wherein lies the essence of Shakespeare's greatness? Certainly not in inventiveness of plot and narrative line; as we know, Shakespeare readily and substantially borrowed the framework of his plays from other sources. Nor does it lie in the themes which the plays set before us, for these – no matter how compellingly germane to our human condition – may be found elsewhere. Our answer must be that Shakespeare's greatness is rooted in his language, a language which can shift by turn from ribald commonplace to stately artifice, to awesome passion, to the sublimest beauty. And all with a sure rightness of expression which, at its best, takes possession of the heart and mind to assert with clinching certainty that the words before us could not possibly be phrased in any other way.

The greatness is in the poetry. Yet the characters of the plays are not simply mouthers of poetry, the deliverers of a sequence of poetic artefacts; indeed they *are* the poetry, the poetry is the means by which they grow in our minds, by which we come to know them. The speaker and his language may not be separated. Nor should we forget that for all this glorious language, which so richly repays attentive study, we are dealing with *plays*, not extended poems with moving characters, but theatrical experiences. A powerful corrective against the 'long poem syndrome' is to consider that Shakespeare's plays are marked by extensive use of *prose*, which in the case of *King Lear* amounts to some twenty-five per cent of the text.

A broadly acceptable generalisation would be that Shakespeare regarded prose as a medium of comedy. Yet in great tragedies such as *Lear*, *Hamlet* and *Coriolanus,* Shakespeare's use of prose is significant – and not just for intermittent comic relief.

Would Shakespeare's audiences have noted *aurally* the shifts between verse and prose? Most certainly, for not only are they likely to have been more sensitive to such transitions than we are, but the mode of delivery by the actors would have emphasised it; the verse would have been spoken in an essentially stylised manner, with insistent rhythmic stress. Elizabethan audiences would also have been aware of the conventions which governed differential use of verse and prose. Prose was regularly used for letters and proclamations impinging upon the action of the play. More fundamentally, because prose was recognised as a less refined medium than verse, it was associated with the speeches and activities of characters deemed to be below the dignity of verse: servants, clowns, villains, madmen. Even when a noble character of central importance speaks prose – *and this often happens* – it will usually be because that character is in some sense being debased, or is shown in an unusually relaxed context. Because of its sense of 'apartness', prose is regularly established as the medium for a sub-plot. The critic Elisabeth Tschopp has a useful definition:

> to verse is allotted the noble, eminent and heroic-romantic sphere; the concentrated state of affairs; the purposeful, momentous and tragic action; truth, dignity, order; the poetic word; the universally applicable generalisation; the official, solemn occasion; passionate and demoniacal feelings. To prose, on the other hand, is given the world of sober realism and robust comedy; witty entertainment; playful diversion; delay; dissimulation, degradation, chaos; colloquial speech and incorrect pronunciation. (*Prosa in Shakespeares Dramen*, Schweizer Anglistische Arbeiten, Bern, 1956)

In *King Lear*, substantial use of prose is given to Lear himself, to Gloucester, Edmund, Edgar, Kent and the Fool – and always for a reason. Some claim that the shifts into prose are essentially haphazard, that they represent the 'unfixed' and destabilised world of the play, but this is surely naive. When Shakespeare gives his characters prose to speak, he does so for reasons of dramatic contrast, to achieve some significant juxtaposition with the standard medium of verse.

Let us examine some examples. The 'men of the world' conversation between Kent and Gloucester at the beginning of the play is rightly in prose, and provides a fine contrast with Lear's ceremonial verse. When Goneril and Regan return to prose at the end of the scene, it marks the end of the public context and hints at their harsh realism and deceitfulness. Gloucester, the rather bumbling and tentative old man, speaks prose, but is elevated to verse in the pathos of his suffering. In Act I.ii, Edmund's exultant hymning of his own amorality at the beginning and the end of the scene is in verse, yet the actual gulling of father and brother is in prose. Kent as the impassioned courtier in the first scene naturally speaks verse, but becomes Kent, the plain man of prose, as he serves the master who cast him out; yet when after III.i his devotion to Lear becomes more tenderly solicitous, he returns to verse. As we would expect, The Fool speaks prose – as do those who banter with him; yet note the fine effect of the storm scene (III.ii) where Lear's tormented verse is set against the comic prose of the Fool, thus emphasising the isolated anguish of the king. Naturally, Lear declines into prose in his madness, but when occasionally he rises out of it, the effect is telling; an example is considered in Chapter 5. Like Edmund and Kent, Edgar adopts prose for the purposes of concealment when he assumes a mask of madness; his occasional verse asides and verse soliloquies (II.iii, III.vi, IV.i) are necessary reminders that he remains the refined and dignified nobleman. Consider also that, as with Kent, Edgar reverts to verse when in IV.i he plays a more overtly supportive role, returning briefly to broad prose as he drubs Oswald. In the *dénouement* of the play, as identities are resumed, some degree of restoration achieved and the full weight of tragedy experienced, verse is re-established as the standard medium.

The transitions vetween verse and prose, far from being random, are an essential and finely judged aspect of the structure of the play. If we are aware of them and of what they stand for – as we should be – our perception of character and situation will be enhanced.

Passionate speech always finds its own rhythm. In acknowledging the rightness of this judgement we will also recognise that it is through the medium of the blank verse of *King Lear* that the mightiest passions and finest feelings are conveyed.

What is the nature, the history of this 'blank verse' about which we talk so readily? Had it long been a traditional feature of English drama and poetry? In fact, it was only in 1557 – seven years before Shakespeare's birth – that the Earl of Surrey, seeking a suitable medium for the rendering of Latin epics in translation, developed the experimental metric form of the iambic pentameter: the ten-syllable line, divided into five pairs (or 'feet') or two syllables – unstressed followed by stressed – with the lines in general unrhymed:

> They whisted all, with fixed face attent
> When Prince Aeneas from the royal seat
> Thus gan to speak, O Queene, it is thy will,
> I should renew a woe cannot be told.

Thus English literature was transformed, and Elizabethan drama given its most characteristic voice.

Just as Shakespeare's use of prose developed throughout his career, so did his verse. In early plays such as *Love's Labour's Lost* we see a marked taste for rhyming couplets, an inclination still present in such 'middle period' plays as *Romeo and Juliet* and *Richard II*.

We see also, perhaps, a tendency for Shakespeare to observe with greater readiness the metric restrictions of his verse form. In the towering plays of the tragic phase we are struck by the rampant flexibility of the verse form. It is as though pressure of felling and heightened emotions demand, and secure, a more liberal metric expression.

Of course, we can point in *King Lear* to examples of regular rhyming couplets - usually to round off a scene or add emphasis to the departure of a character; we may think of Kent's parting words in I.i, of the conclusion of Edmund's scandalous self-revelation at the end of I.ii, or of the words of Edgar which bring the play to a close. Yet is is the blank verse, and in particular its seething variety of form, which claims the attention. 'Run-on' lines are common; extra syllables and part-lines are readily allowed; frequently the line will 'crack' under the weight of feeling. Thus we have a verse form which allows the lofty sweep of:

> To thee and thine, hereditary ever,
> Remain this ample third of our fair kingdom,
> No less in space, validity, and pleasure
> Than that conferred on Goneril. Now, our joy,
> Although our last and least, to whose young love
> The vines of France and milk of Burgundy
> Strive to be interessed, what can you say to draw
> A third more opulent than your sisters? Speak. (I.i.80-7)

the fragmented expostulations of:

> Thou rascal beadle, hold thy bloody hand!
> Why dost thou lash that whore? Strip thy own back;
> Thou hotly lusts to use her in that kind
> For which thou whipp'st her. The usurer hangs the cozener.
> Through tattered clothes great vices do appear;
> Robes and furred gowns hide all. Plate sin with gold,
> And the strong lance of justice hurtless breaks;
> Arm it in rags, a pigmy's straw does pierce it.
> None does offend, none, I say none. I'll able 'em.
> Take that of me, my friend, who have the power
> To seal th'accuser's lips. Get thee glass eyes
> And like a scurvy politician seem
> To see the things thou dost not. Now, now, now, now!
> Pull off my boots. Harder, harder! So. (IV.vi.159-72)

the panting monosyllables (note the end-stopping) of:

> I know when one is dead, and when one lives;
> She's dead as earth. Lend me a looking-glass;
> If that her breath will mist or stain the stone,
> Why, then she lives. (V.iii.260-3)

Far from being a restrictive medium, a matter of correctness and syllable counting, the blank verse of *King Lear* is wonderfully responsive to the feelings expressed.

4.4 IMAGERY

The greatest gift, according to the philosopher Aristotle, is a talent for metaphor, an ability to express penetratingly the essence of a thing, emotion or situation in terms of another, and thus to convey the sharpness of one's own vision and sensitivity to one's reader or spectator. It is a gift possessed in the highest degree by Shakespeare, for much of the greatness of his plays lies in their imagery. In his earlier plays the imagery – always striking and often exquisitely beautiful – is nonetheless often of a conventionally 'decorative' nature'. In the later plays there is little of the merely illustrative or ornamental; the imagery here is more dense, more complex, more *integral* to the emotions and dilemmas of the plays – and to our conception of the characters who live through them. Remember, the characters *are* the poetry.

King Lear, like any play, may be perceived simply on the level of narrative events, but the real riches are reserved for those who can identify and respond to the vibrant web of imagery which underpins both character and incident. In general, the imagery of the play is compelling, dark, harsh, disturbing. There is little here that is beautiful; the description of Cordelia's grief at her father's suffering is one of the few exceptions which prove the rule:

> You have seen
> Sunshine and rain at once; her smiles and tears
> Were like a better way; those happy smilets
> That played on her ripe lip seemed not to know
> What guests were in her eyes, which parted thence
> As pearls from diamonds dropped. (IV.iii.18-23)

Further broadly acceptable generalisations may be made concerning the distribution of the imagery. Some of the characters – Goneril, Regan, Edmund and Cornwall – have very little imagery in their speeches, and how right this is; these are rational, cold and unimaginative people, concerned not with the inner man but with a ruthless pursuit of satisfaction in the material world. Harshly mechanical people for whom imaginative insights and promptings would be out of character. On the other hand, Lear and many of the characters closest to him (the Fool, Kent and Edgar) speak a language rich in imagery, as they grapple to find and transmit shape, pattern and understanding. Lear expresses himself ever more densely in imagery as the play proceeds, to the point where it becomes his most characteristic form of utterance. As we might expect, Acts II-IV are the richest in imagery, for here the recognisable human world of order and pattern breaks down as Lear's anguish escalates into madness. In this section of the play, Lear's words - his imagery - are less a mode of communication with others than a figurative expression of his inner torment.

Characteristic of Shakespeare's imagery, particularly in his mature plays, are patterns of interrelated images which recur through the whole work and reflect its most pressing concerns. We should avoid the temptation to write glibly of these recurring images as if they were 'planted' studiedly at appropriate points in the play as part of a preconceived scheme. That they reappear as they do is an indication of the extent to which certain 'key visualisations' or 'lead symbols' had coloured Shakespeare's imagination as he wrote. We do not have time or space for an extensive catalogue of such recurring images, but some brief examples will point the way:

(a) When Lear divides his kingdom, he splits not only his country but his family, his court and, ultimately, his mind. Consider how images of cracking/breaking/shattering resound throughout the play:

   i) Gloucester picks up the image almost immediately:

> Love cools, friendship falls off, brothers divide.
> In cities, mutinies; in countries, discord; in palaces, treason;
> and the bond cracked 'twixt son and father. (I.ii.110-13)

   ii) Convinced of Edgar's treachery, Gloucester cries:

> O! Madam, my old heart is crack'd, it's crack'd. (II.i.90)

   iii) Seeing at last the treachery of both daughters, Lear's despair echoes the theme:

> I have full cause of weeping, but this heart
> Shall break into a hundred thousand flaws
> Or ere I'll weep. (II.iv.282-4)

   iv) Exposed to the storm, Lear demands that the heavens shatter a wicked world. We think of:

> Blow, winds, and crack your cheeks! (III.ii.1)

and

> Strike flat the thick rotundity o'th'world,
> Crack Nature's moulds (III.ii.7-8)

v) Reconciled with Edgar, Albany asserts:

> Let sorrow split my heart if ever I
> Did hate thee or thy father. (V.iii.176-7)

vi) Gloucester's death is couched in similar terms:

> his flawed heart,
> (Alack, too weak the conflict to support)
> 'Twixt two extremes of passion, joy and grief,
> Burst smilingly. (V.iii.195-8)

vii) The report of Kent's emotional account of his master's suffering carries on the echo:

> in recounting
> His grief grew puissant, and the strings of life
> Began to crack. (V.iii.214-16)

These few examples represent an important line of imagery – and one highly appropriate in a play dominated by disruption, dislocation and emotional chaos.

(b) If, as already observed, Acts II-IV are particularly dense with imagery, it will be discerned that it is essentially the non-human imagery of the world of nature. Accepted bonds are destroyed, traditional human patterns and practices are set aside, and Lear finds himself on the heath. There is no place now for imagery rooted in accepted modes of human society; instead, Lear's mind is seared by imagery of animals and plants and particularly of the frenzied elements: lightning, thunder, rain and wind.

(c) Animal imagery represents one of the most compelling patterns in the play, thrusting before us constantly the bestiality of Goneril and Regan. For the statistically minded, it has been observed that the play contains 133 separate mentions of sixty-four different animals. More important is for us to observe that our minds are repeatedly directed to the claws, the teeth, the beak, the sting, the bite of these animals. Not only are our minds forced to dwell on the sub-human evil which torments Lear and Gloucester, but also more specifically on the raking sharpness with which they are lacerated in mind and body.

(d) The unnaturalness of Lear's rashness in I.i and then of the foul cruelty to which he is exposed is embodied in a sequence of disease imagery. Kent initiates this with:

> Kill thy physician, and thy fee bestow
> Upon the foul disease. (I.i.164-5)

It then reappears intermittently throughout the play:

> a disease that's in my flesh,
> Which I must needs call mine. Thou art a boil,
> A plague-sore, or embossed carbuncle
> In my corrupted blood. (II.iv.220-3)

This line of imagery finds its natural conclusion in the healing presence of the doctor in IV.vii.

(e) The imagery of clothing is significant. In the early stages, fine clothing represents power and status; we think of Lear's references to his daughters' splendid apparel in his 'Reason not the need' speech. The tearing off of his sodden rags to join Poor Tom in muddy nakedness symbolises Lear's striving for the basic core of humanity, while his brief rebirth in IV.vii is reflected in the almost baptismal quality of his fresh garments.

(f) The imagery of 'nothing' demands attention. It begins with the sharp interchange between Lear and Cordelia:

CORDELIA	Nothing, my lord.
LEAR	Nothing?
CORDLIA	Nothing.
LEAR	Nothing will come of nothing (I.i.88-91)

Nothing is, indeed, what Cordelia and Edgar are left with, but soon the word moves away from the realm of possessions to take on connotations of personal identity, one's grasp of who and what one is. The Fool drives the point home to Lear: 'now thou art an O without a figure. I am better than thou art now; I am a Fool, thou art nothing' (I.iv.193-5). Edgar projects this annihilation of identity when he becomes Poor Tom: 'Edgar I nothing am' (II.iii.21). It is only when Lear is and has nothing – when he strips off his clothes to become a naked nothing – that he truly reaches the pit of the abyss from which redemption becomes a possibility.

(g) In a play which stems from the inability of two old men to see into themselves and others, it is hardly surprising that one of the dominant lines of imagery is to do with eyes and sight, darkness and light. We can look only at a brief sample. With bitter irony, Goneril assures Lear that she loves him 'Dearer than eyesight' (I.i.57). When Lear clashes with Kent, he orders him 'Out of my sight!' only to receive the retort 'See better, Lear' (I.i.158-9). In I.iv the Fool prefigures the gathering gloom in 'So out went the candle and we were left darkling' (I.iv.219), while a few lines later, Lear is asking of himself 'Where are his eyes?' (228). In II.iv the Fool explores the theme further:

> Fathers that wear rags
> Do make their children blind,
> But fathers that bear bags
> Shall see their children kind. (47-50)

Ironically, it is in the darkness of the night, when virtually nothing external can be seen, that Lear begins to fumble his way back to moral sight. As the doctor aptly observes, he has many herbs which will help to 'close the eye of anguish' (IV.iv.15). Nor will we miss the poignancy of Lear's remark as he bends over the corpse of Cordelia:

> Mine eyes are not o'th'best (V.iii.279)

The blinding of Gloucester is a bitter culmination of a career in which clearsightedness regarding his own moral standards and his judgement of his sons has been notably absent. The scene in which Regan and Cornwall confront and then torture Gloucester is packed with the imagery of eyes and sight, and thereafter we must endure the bitter irony that, blinded, he now begins to 'see':

> I have no way and therefore want no eyes;
> I stumbled when I saw. (IV.i.18-19)

Moral understanding sharpens apace, as he expounds a new view of the world, again hinging on sight imagery:

> Let the superfluous and lust-dieted man,
> That slaves your ordinance, that will not see
> Because he does not feel, feel your power quickly. (IV.i.67-9)

Of course, there is more, much more, that could be quoted, but we have examined enough to appreciate the resonance of Edgar's closing lines:

> we that are young
> Shall never see so much. . .

Above all, this is a play about how we should assess and weigh accurately - *see clearly* - in our dealings with others.

It must be understood that recurring patterns of imagery in the play - far from being mere verbal adornment of its themes and concerns - are the means by which we feel and relate to them.

4.5 **STAGECRAFT**

We should constantly remind ourselves that *King Lear* is a play, with all the spectacle, variety of stage presence and audience involvement that this implies – the 'two hours' traffic of our stage' referred to in *Romeo and Juliet*.

To grasp the significance of visual impact in the play, we need only consider such varied scenes as Lear's majestic entry in I.i; the deranged ceremonial of the mad 'trial'; the blinding of Gloucester and his duping at the imaginary cliff edge; the serene tableau of Lear waking in the care of Cordelia; the ritualistic spectacle of the duel; Lear's entry with the dead Cordelia. Truly, the play demands to be seen.

As for audience involvement, note how frequently we experience suspense and foreboding, as, for instance, we anticipate anxiously Lear's passionate response to the sisters' cruelty; as Gloucester confides in the son who will ruin him; as Cornwall swears revenge; as the gentleman enters with the bloody knife; as Edmund reveals, too late, his fatal instructions. We can only appreciate such suspense by seeing or visualising the play, and by doing so as if for the *first* time. Drama hinges on conflict, and we recognise also the innate power of such scenes as Lear's clash with Cordelia and Kent; his cursing of Goneril and Regan; the servant's attack on Cornwall; Albany's confronting of Goneril and Edmund. Given our identification with the characters, these episodes represent genuinely stirring theatrical experiences.

A further consideration is the skilful manipulation of atmosphere on stage. Reading a play, we may put down the book. In the theatre our response requires variety of scene and mood, and so we have intermittent humour: the manhandling of Oswald, Kent's mockery of Cornwall, the prattle of the Fool. We also have regular alternation of mood, in such juxtapositions as the high rage of I.iv succeeded by the pained calm of I.v; the stormy heath alongside the sinister quiet of the castle; Cordelia's love in IV.iv followed by Regan's lust in IV.v; the killing of Oswald and the discovery of Goneril's letter preceding Lear's hesitant awakening. This variation is paralleled by the range of *sound* against which the action takes place: the Fool's snatches of song, the discord of the storm, the harmonies which soothe Lear, the clash of battle, the howls of a broken old man.

As readers of the play, we rejoice in its glorious language, its characterisation, its thematic concerns; as spectators, our eyes and ears are engaged as well as our imaginations – and our fulfilment is all the greater.

5 SPECIMEN CRITICAL ANALYSIS

LEAR   No, they cannot touch me for coining; I am
        the king himself.
EDGAR   O thou side-piercing sight!
LEAR   Nature's above art in that respect. There's
        your press-money. That fellow handles his bow
        like a crow-keeper; draw me a clothier's yard.
        Look, look, a mouse! Peace, peace; this piece
        of toasted cheese will do't. There's my gauntlet;
        I'll prove it on a giant. Bring up the brownbills.
        O, well-flown, bird; i'th'clout, i'th'clout:
        hewgh! Give the word.
EDGAR   Sweet marjoram.
LEAR   Pass
GLOUCESTER   I know that voice
LEAR   Ha! Goneril with a white beard? They flattered
        me like a dog and told me I had the white hairs in
        my beard ere the black ones were there. To say
        'ay' and 'no' to everything that I said! 'Ay'
        and 'no' too, was no good divinity. When the
        rain came to wet me once and the wind to make me
        chatter, when the thunder would not peace at my
        bidding, there I found'em' there I smelt ' em
        out! Go to, they are not men o'their words.
        They told me I was everything; tis a lie – I am
        not ague-proof.
GLOUCESTER   The trick of that voice I do well
              remember:
              Is't not the King?
LEAR   Ay, every inch a King!
        When I do stare, see how the subject quakes.
        I pardon that man's life. What was thy cause?
        Adultery?
        Thou shalt not die. Die for adultery? No!

The wren goes to't, and the small gilded fly
Does lecher in my sight.
Let copulation thrive: for Gloucester's bastard son
Was kinder to his father than my daughters
Got 'tween the lawful sheets.
To't, luxury, pell-mell! for I lack soldiers.
Behold yon simpering dame
Whose face between her forks presages snow,
That minces virtue and does shake the head
To hear of pleasure's name;
The fitchew nor the soiled horse goes to't
With a more riotous appetite.
Down from the waist they are centaurs,
Though women all above.
But to the girdle do the gods inherit,
Beneath is all the fiend's.
There's hell, there's darkness, there is the
sulphurous pit;
Burning, scalding, stench, consumption: fie, fie,
fie, pah, pah!
Give me an ounce of civet; good apothecary,
sweeten my imagination. There's money for thee.

(Iv.vi.83–131)

Gloucester has just been duped by Edgar into believing that he has been
providentially saved following a fall from Dover cliffs. The affirmative
mood of his victory over despair is checked by the arrival of a deranged
Lear, decked with wild flowers. In this, Lear's last mad appearance, we
note the structural significance of the bringing together of the two wronged
fathers, the blind and the mad.

As we would expect in view of his madness, Lear is speaking prose.
We last saw him at the end of the crazed trial scene in Gloucester's outhouse. Perhaps this accounts for the continuing legalistic tone of 'they
cannot touch me': the idea of charges and accusations is still in his mind.
Yet we note his re-assertion of his kingship. He, unlike the others (Goneril?
Regan? Cornwall?), is no sham. He is the thing itself. No forgery ('coining')
in his case. 'Nature's above art' clinches his confidence. He is a king *naturally*;
they (by 'art') have been 'manufactured'. Edgar's bewailing of the spectacle as 'side-piercing sight' is important, for it reduces the possibility of
audience amusement at Lear's appearance and prattle.

Lear's wandering monologue (86–92) is a masterly rendering of a
madman's babble: dislocated ideas and visions, tenuously linked by
fluttering association of ideas. The 'unfixed' quality of his mind is conveyed by the broken structure of the prose. In just seven lines, there are
some fourteen units of thought or feeling. 'Coining' seems to have provoked 'press money' (because of the stamping or pressing involved in
making a coin), which calls to mind the recruit at target practice with his

bow. The insulting jibe of 'crow-keeper' – a scarecrow or boy employed to frighten away the crows – may suggest a mouse found in a field of crops. 'Peace' may be suggested by lingering ideas of war, or a desire not to frighten the tiny creature. 'Peace' leads to 'piece' and the cheese which the mouse would enjoy. We are back to battle with the challenge of the gauntlet, perhaps to 'prove' the kingship asserted at the beginning? Maybe the 'giant' as an imaginary opponent is suggested by juxtaposition with the tiny mouse. With 'brown bills' (halberds) we are back to soldiers, but 'bills' suggest birds,which then become arrows firing at the target, thus returning us to the archery of the recruits. Soldiers and soldiering resound through this speech; Lear's subconscious is still not free of the retinue to which he once attached so much importance.

Edgar humours Lear by providing a password: once more the soother, the bringer of peace. Consider also that 'sweet marjoram' was regarded as a cure for mental disturbance.

'Goneril with a white beard!' is a reflection of how much she still preys on his mind. Note it is Goneril rather than Regan: the former even more detestable than the latter. We see Lear's precise insight into how badly he had been flattered and misled. This understanding from a mad-man? The mental clouds are beginning to clear.

There is tension throughout this speech between the first person 'I/me/my' and the manipulating 'they' and "em'. We see also, as elsewhere, the image of the dog as a fawning creature, and the white beard as the symbol of venerable wisdom. There is no deranged rambling here; Goneril suggests lies and flattery, which reminds Lear of how he had been con-trolled by sycophants, which in turn leads him to recall his moment of truth, the agony on the heath when he realised his own fragility. From 'When the rain . . .', the sentences build up a cumulative rhythm, partly dependent on balance and repetition: 'When . . . when', 'there I . . .there I'. The climax of his discovery is well conveyed by the emphatic tri-partite insistence of 'Go to . . . They told me . . . 'tis a lie'.

Lear at last now perceives the truth and it is fitting that his discovery of those who deceived him is an *implied* continuation of the animal imagery which has always characterised them: 'there I found 'em, there I smelt 'em out.' There is a curiously vague and child-like quality about 'When the rain came to wet me once and the wind to make me chatter': there is no precision of time or place, as though he recalls it through a painful haze. The climax of the speech, 'I am not ague-proof', may be under-stood on several levels:

(a) I am not invincible and all-powerful, as I was once flatteringly per-suaded;

(b) I was physically vulnerable to the bleakness of the heath;

(c) (remembering the disease imagery which symbolises evil), I was not able to resist immorality and maliciousness.

Gloucester's recognition of his master reasserts the regal status with which the passage opened. The alacrity with which Lear 'accepts the crown', just a line or so after his stark self-awareness, points to his continuing instability. As he begins to act the monarch, he appropriately shifts to verse, glorying in power and dispensing lofty fiats; the lingering idea of the courtroom is still in his subconscious, presumably because his fevered mind remains concerned with sorting out good from evil, true from false, innocent from guilty.

The elaborate posturing of Lear's amazement that anyone should die for adultery is transmitted by the fragmented line structure. This speech is heavily coloured by the diction of sexual licence and revulsion: 'adultery', 'goes to't', 'lecher', 'copulation', 'bastard', 'luxury', 'fitchew', 'riotous appetite', 'centaurs'. As Sigmund Freud, the great psychiatrist, was to show some three hundred years later, such disgust is often characteristic of mental disturbance. The universe is viewed through the prism of the foulness to which Lear has himself been subjected, and he sees evil and self-indulgence everywhere. Again the idea of right and wrong is captured in 'bastard son' as opposed to 'lawful sheets', though here Gloucester will wince, for he now knows the truth about Edmund. 'For I lack soldiers' may be construed on the one hand as a reason for unfettered promiscuity, for this would lead to recruits in plenty; alternatively, it may simply be a distracted memory which continues to haunt him.

The reference to 'my daughters' is a moment of piercing clarity and real pain. It must be this thought which calls forth the bitter tirade against the prim posing and covert lust of woman. The 'simp'ring dame' sequence picks up the recurrent theme of hypocrisy. 'Forks' may refer to hairslides or combs, but more probably the reference is to legs and the false promise of sexual restraint. From 'Behold yond' to 'pleasure's name' there is a rhythmic accumulation on the supposed chastity of this archetypal woman, which is then viciously dispelled as we plunge into 'The fitchew nor the soiled horse'. Again animals represent baseness in human conduct, though 'fitchew' was also a colloquialism for a prostitute.

The pace escalates with the poised opposites of 'centaurs'/'women' and 'Gods'/'fiend', and now the structure breaks down under the pressure of Lear's tempestuous loathing. We have a series of ranting ejaculations, of demonic word-associations ('fiend', 'hell', 'darkness', 'sulphurous pit', 'burning', 'scalding', 'stench', 'consumption'), until in the end words give way to hawking and spitting as Lear turns aside and tries to clear his mind and mouth of the filth that torments him.

Then, suddenly, he is more calm as – again in the ordinariness of prose – he delivers his courteous request to an imagined apothecary. Perhaps this vision of a man dealing in herbs and potions is a reflection of a deep-seated understanding that he is in need of healing. The diction of 'civet', 'apothecary' and 'sweeten' does much to soothe Lear, and us, after his turbulent outburst.

Finally, as Lear offers to pay for his order, we are back with the idea of *money*, which is how the extract began. After much anguished rambling – with moments of penetrating clarity – Lear's consciousness has found its way back to the preoccupation with which he was grappling as he entered.

6 CRITICAL APPRAISALS

To read the considered opinions of a sensitive and intelligent critic can be both a profit and a delight. Our eyes may be opened to something we have missed; we may enjoy a fresh perspective on a familiar theme; a nagging problem of interpretation may be dispelled. In short, our response may be heightened and refined.

Equally, however, a critic's views may be ill-founded, biased or exaggerated. Byron, who had no time for the breed, was typically scathing:

> . . . As soon
> Seek roses in December – ice in June:
> Hope constancy in wind, or corn in chaff;
> Believe a woman or an epitaph,
> Or any other thing that's false, before
> You trust in critics.
> (*English Bards and Scotch Reviewers*)

Critics – and women – may well protest at such an exaggeration, but there is an important point here. Critical opinions are not gospel truth, to be cherished and revered – certainly not to be memorised slavishly and produced as clinching evidence in an essay. They represent simply the judgements of individual men and women, worth no more, innately, than your own views. Read as much critical comment as you can, but retain a healthy scepticism. Be prepared to modify your views in the light of what you read, but remain independent – and reach your own conclusions.

King Lear received comparatively little critical attention before the nineteenth century. Addison (1711), Joseph Warton (1753) and Richardson (1784) wrote interestingly enough about the play, but the most celebrated comment from this period came in 1765 from Samuel Johnson: 'I was many years ago so shocked by Cordelia's death, that I know not whether I ever endured to read again the last scenes of the play till I undertook to revise them as an editor'.

Perhaps this lent a certain legitimacy to the absurdity of Tate's 'happy ending' version, which from 1681 held sway on the stage for nearly a century and a half, until attacked by, among others, Lamb.

The play certainly had its fervent admirers:

King Lear . . . may be judged the most perfect specimen of the dramatic art existing in the world. (Shelley, 1821)

the most tremendous effort of Shakespeare as a poet. (Coleridge, 1822)

the tragedy of the old king constitutes the mightiest, the vastest, the most stirring, the most intense dramatic poem that has ever been written. (Maeterlinck, 1905)

Nor are eminent opponents hard to find. Tolstoy preferred Shakespeare's source:

However strange this opinion may seem to worshippers of Shakespeare, yet the whole of this old drama is incomparably and in every respect superior to Shakespeare's adaptation. It is so, firstly, because it has not got the utterly superfluous characters of the villain Edmund and the unlifelike Gloucester and Edgar, who only distract one's attention; secondly, because it has not got the completely false effects of Lear running about the heath, his conversations with the fool and all these impossible disguises, failures to recognise, and accumulated deaths. (Tolstoy, 1907)

Save for a few beauties of lyrical eloquence . . . all the rest is no more than a heap of stupid crimes, foolish horrors and idiotic vices . . . almost anybody, no matter who, could write *King Lear*. (Faguet, 1905)

One wicked daughter would have been quite enough, and Edgar is a superfluous character. (George Orwell, 1950)

Even its devotees have had doubts about the play in performance. Lamb felt that *Lear* was an experience for the study, rather than the theatre:

But the *Lear* of Shakespeare cannot be acted. The contemptible machinery by which they mimic the storm which he goes out in, is not more inadequate to represent the horrors of the real elements, than any actor can be to present Lear. (1811)

In 1904, A. C. Bradley would agree:

The stage is the test of dramatic quality, and *King Lear* is too huge for the stage.

Granville Barker, however, was in no doubt: '*King Lear* was meant to be acted' (1927); and Spencer affirmed that the play demands to be *seen*:

> The scenes on the heath . . . should be imagined in relation to the opening of the play; the contrast of visual impression, the contrast of tableau, must be concretely perceived by the eye as the contrast of rhythm and word by the ear. (1942)

These comments serve to indicate the varying critical evaluation of *King Lear*, and the danger of trusting too much in any one judgement just because it is in print!

Since the restoration of its textual integrity in the mid-nineteenth century, the play has become a focus of continuing critical attention. There follows, without further supporting comment, a small selection of 'expert' opinion. Let the critics speak:

> the process of degradation is always the same. Everything that distinguishes a man – his titles, social position, even name – is lost. Names are not needed any more. Everyone is just a shadow of himself; just a man. (Jan Kott, 1964)

> Throughout that stupendous Third Act the good are seen growing better through suffering, and the bad worse through success. The warm castle is a room in hell, the storm-swept heath a sanctuary.
> (A. C. Bradley, 1904)

> Recurrent throughout the play is the sense that the breaking of human ties, especially ties of close blood or plighted loyalty, is so abnormal and unnatural that it must be a symptom of some dread convulsion in the frame of things. (Enid Welsford, 1935)

> To follow the master, to sustain the state, to bless one's child, to succour the aged and one's parents – this idea of being brought back to rectitude is what the play ends with. (John Holloway, 1961)

> a stony black despairing depth of voiceless and inexplicable agony.
> (J. A. Symonds, 1883)

> There is in fact poetic justice enough in *King Lear*. Goneril, Regan, Cornwall and Edmund, all perish in their sins. Evil is destroyed.
> (C. J. Sisson, 1962)

> It seems almost beyond question that any actor is false to the text who does not attempt to express, in Lear's last accents and gestures and look, an unbearable joy. (A. C. Bradley)

Shakespeare opposes the presence and the influence of evil not by any transcendental denial of evil, but by the presence of human virtue, fidelity and self-sacrificial love. (A. C. Bradley)

In this play alone among the tragedies we are asked to take seriously literal disguises that deceive. (Maynard Mack, 1965)

Of the twelve major characters half are just and good; the other half, unjust and bad. It is a division as consistent and abstract as in a morality play. (Jan Kott)

On the whole, and this is true of other plays beside *King Lear*, Shakespeare tends to give more intellectual ability to his sinners than to his saints. Edmund, for instance, is so shrewd and witty that he almost wins our sympathy for his unabashed cruelty. (Enid Welsford)

Edmund is given a noble, an essentially tragic end, and Goneril and Regan, too, meet their ends with something of tragic fineness in pursuit of their evil desires . . . They die, at least, in the cause of love – love of Edmund. (G. Wilson Knight, 1930)

The principal structural weakness of *King Lear* . . . arises chiefly from the double action. (A. C. Bradley)

Lear, without questioning his own rightness, imposes his will upon others; Gloucester accepts the will of others without effectually questioning their rightness. (Robert B. Heilman, 1948)

the play moves us by sympathy for Lear: and that sympathy is created by poetry. (Barbara Everett, 1960)

the general 'floating' image, kept constantly before us, chiefly by means of the verbs used, but also in metaphor, of a human body in anguished movement, tugged, wrenched, beaten, pierced, stung, scourged, dislocated, flayed, gashed, scalded, tortured, and finally broken on the rack. (C.F.E. Spurgeon, 1935)

King Lear, a play set in the legendary pre-history of Britain, depicts a world which is remote and primaeval. This is not to deny that it has life and meaning for all times: its permanent relevance is what follows from having the quality of legend, and the primaeval as subject.

(John Holloway)

A tremendous soul is, as it were, incongruously geared to a puerile intellect . . . Lear is mentally a child, in passion a titan. (G. Wilson Knight)

Should we not be ... near the truth, if we called this poem 'The Redemption of King Lear', and declared that the business of 'the gods' with him was neither to torment him, nor to teach him a 'noble anger', but to lead him to attain through apparently hopeless failure the very end and aim of life? (A. C. Bradley)

The 'clothing' that is removed in the first part of the play is that of traditional assurances of position, home and family; it is replaced in Act IV by a clothing of ideas, of justice and redemption. When that too is stripped in Act V, we are left alone with exhaustion and the relief of death. The concepts fade away, but the naked experience remains. (Nicholas Brooke, 1963)

As we draw near to the awful close of *King Lear* . . . and feel the fibres of our being almost torn asunder, the comfort that comes to us when quiet falls on the desolate scene is the comfort of the sure knowledge that Shakespeare is with us; that he who saw these things felt them as we do, and found in the splendours of courage and love a remedy for despair. (Raleigh, 1901)

QUESTIONS

1. 'The parallels between Lear and Gloucester should not blind us to the enormous differences between them.' Discuss.

2. Illustrate and explore the varied meanings of 'Nature' in the play.

3. We often read of the 'cosmic scale' of *King Lear*. How is this achieved?

4. 'The characters are too extreme, too stereotyped.' Discuss.

5. Consider the proposition that film is the only medium which can convey the fullness of *King Lear*.

6. An innocent daughter and 'a man more sinned against than sinning'. What is the dramatic justification for the deaths of Cordelia and Lear?

7. 'The actor's difficulty is that he must start upon a top note . . . yet have in reserve the means to a greater climax' (Granville Barker). *Is* Lear an exceptionally demanding role? Explain.

8. Comment on the play's treatment of the theme of justice.

9. 'The pre-historic context is irrelevant; the play would lose nothing from being set in, say, the medieval period.' How far do you agree with this judgement?

10. 'It is too easy to condemn Goneril, Regan, Edmund and Cornwall. They are not entirely reprehensible.' Make out a case for the defence.

11. 'Both plot and characterisation are banal; the play's real glory is its poetry.' Discuss this judgement of *King Lear*.

12. 'We are often assured of the Fool's functional importance in the play. Perhaps so – but in performance he is an overstated irritant.' Comment on this view.

APPENDIX :

SHAKESPEARE'S THEATRE

We should speak, as Muriel Bradbrook reminds us, not of the Elizabethan stage but of Elizabethan stages. Plays of Shakespeare were acted on tour, in the halls of mansions, one at least in Gray's Inn, frequently at Court, and after 1609 at the Blackfrairs, a small, roofed theatre for those who could afford the price. But even after his Company acquired the Blackfriars, we know of no play of his not acted (unless, rather improbably, *Troilus* is an exception) for the general public at the Globe, or before 1599 at its predecessor, The Theatre, which, since the Globe was constructed from the same timbers, must have resembled it. Describing the Globe, we can claim therefore to be describing, in an acceptable sense, Shakespeare's theatre, the physical structure his plays were designed to fit. Even in the few probably written for a first performance elsewhere, adaptability to that structure would be in his mind.

For the facilities of the Globe we have evidence from the drawing of the Swan theatre (based on a sketch made by a visitor to London about 1596) which depicts the interior of another public theatre; the builder's contract for the Fortune theatre, which in certain respects (fortunately including the dimensions and position of the stage) was to copy the Globe; indications in the dramatic texts; comments, like Ben Jonson's on the throne let down from above by machinery; and eye-witness testimony to the number of spectators (in round figures, 3000) accommodated in the auditorium.

In communicating with the audience, the actor was most favourably placed. Soliloquising at the centre of the front of the great platform, he was at the mid-point of the theatre, with no one among the spectators more than sixty feet away from him. That platform-stage (Figs I and II) was the most important feature for performance at the Globe. It had the audience – standing in the yard (10) and seated in the galleries (9) – on three sides of it. It was 43 feet wide, and 27½ feet from front to back. Raised (?5½ feet) above the level of the yard, it had a trap-door (II.8) giving access to the space below it. The actors, with their equipment, occupied the 'tiring house' (attiring-house: 2) immediately at the back of

SHAKESPEARE'S THEATRE

The stage and its adjuncts; the tiring-house; and the auditorium.

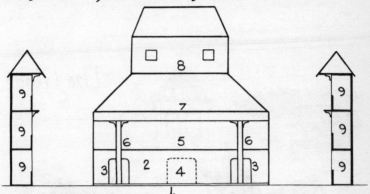

FIG I ELEVATION

1. Platform stage (approximately five feet above the ground) 2. Tiring-house
3. Tiring-house doors to stage 4. Conjectured third door 5. Tiring-house
gallery (balustrade and partitioning not shown) 6. Pillars supporting the
heavens 7. The heavens 8. The hut 9. The spectators' galleries

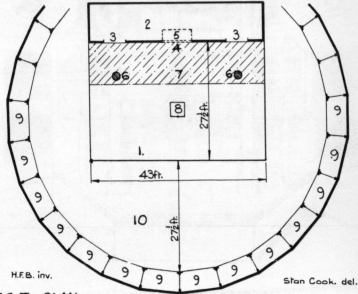

H.F.B. inv.

Stan Cook. del.

FIG II PLAN

1. Platform stage 2. Tiring-house 3. Tiring-house doors to stage
4. Conjectural third door 5. Conjectural discovery space (alternatively behind 3)
6. Pillars supporting the heavens 7. The heavens 8. Trap door 9. Spectators'
gallery 10. The yard

The Globe

An artist's imaginative recreation of a typical Elizabethan theatre

the stage. The stage-direction 'within' means inside the tiring-house. Along its frontage, probably from the top of the second storey, juts out the canopy or 'Heavens', carried on two large pillars rising through the platform (6, 7) and sheltering the rear part of the stage, the rest of which, like the yard, was open to the sky. If the 'hut' (I.8), housing the machinery for descents, stood, as in the Swan drawing, above the 'Heavens', that covering must have had a trap-door, so that the descents could be made through it.

Descents are one illustration of the vertical dimension the dramatist could use to supplement the playing-area of the great platform. The other opportunities are provided by the tiring-house frontage or facade. About this facade the evidence is not as complete or clear as we should like, so that Fig. I is in part conjectural. Two doors giving entry to the platform there certainly were (3). A third (4) is probable but not certain. When curtained, a door, most probably this one, would furnish what must be termed a discovery-space (II.5), not an inner stage (on which action in any depth would have been out of sight for a significant part of the audience). Usually no more than two actors were revealed (exceptionally, three), who often then moved out on to the platform. An example of this is Ferdinand and Miranda in *The Tempest* 'discovered' at chess, then seen on the platform speaking with their fathers. Similarly the gallery (I.5) was not an upper stage. Its use was not limited to the actors: sometimes it functioned as 'lords' rooms' for favoured spectators, sometimes, perhaps, as a musician's gallery. Frequently the whole gallery would not be needed for what took place aloft: a window-stage (as in the first balcony scene in *Romeo*, even perhaps in the second) would suffice. Most probably this would be a part (at one end) of the gallery itself; or just possibly, if the gallery did not (as it does in the Swan drawing) extend the whole width of the tiring-house, a window over the left or right-hand door. As the texts show, whatever was presented aloft, or in the discovery-space, was directly related to the action on the platform, so that at no time was there left, between the audience and the action of the drama, a great bare space of platform-stage. In relating Shakespeare's drama to the physical conditions of the theatre, the primacy of that platform is never to be forgotten.

Note: The present brief account owes most to C. Walter Hodges, *The Globe Restored*; Richard Hosley in *A New Companion to Shakespeare Studies*, and in *The Revels History of English Drama*; and to articles by Hosley and Richard Southern in *Shakespeare Survey*, 12, 1959, where full discussion can be found.

HAROLD BROOKS

FURTHER READING

The Text
Edwards, P. (ed.) *King Lear* (The Macmillan Shakespeare, 1975).
Muir, K.(ed.) *King Lear* (The Arden Shakespeare, Methuen, 1975).

Shakespeare's Life
Schoenbaum, S., *William Shakespeare: A Documentary Life* (Oxford University Press, 1975).
Rowse, A. L., *William Shakespeare* (Macmillan, 1963).
Burgess, A., *Shakespeare* (Cape, 1970).

Criticism
Bradley, A. C., *Shakespearean Tragedy* (Macmillan, 1904; paperback, 1957).
Brooke, N., *Shakespeare: King Lear* (Arnold, 1963).
Campbell, L. B., *Shakespeare's Tragic Heroes* (Methuen, 1961).
Clemen, W. H., *The Development of Shakespeare's Imagery* (Methuen, 1951).
Gardner, H., *King Lear* (London University Press, 1967).
Granville-Barker, H., *Prefaces to Shakespeare* (Batsford, 1963).
Holloway, J., *The Story of the Night* (Routledge & Kegan Paul, 1961).
Jorgensen, P. A., *Lear's Self-discovery* (California University Press, 1967).
Kermode, F. (ed.) *King Lear Casebook* (Macmillan, 1969).
Knight, G. W., *The Wheel of Fire* (Methuen, 1954).
Knights, L. C., *Some Shakespearean Themes* (Chatto & Windus, 1959).
Sisson, C. F., *Shakespeare's Tragic Justice* (Methuen, 1962).
Somerville, H., *Madness in Shakespearean Tragedy* (Richards Press, 1929).
Speaight, R., *Nature in Shakespearean Tragedy* (Hollis & Carter, 1955).
Spurgeon, C., *Shakespeare's Imagery and What It Tells Us* (Cambridge University Press, 1935).
Stauffer, D., *Shakespeare's World of Images* (New York, 1949).